SPECIAL
REPORT

September 2015
Executive Intelligence Review

'Global Warming' Scare Is Population Reduction, Not Science

Edited by Paul Gallagher and Jason Ross

Written by Marcia Merry Baker, Alicia Cerretani, Benjamin Deniston, Liona Fan-Chiang, Paul Gallagher, Jeffrey Steinberg, and Helga Zepp-LaRouche

Typography by Alan Yue

Publication and distribution by Bob Bowen

Executive Intelligence Review
P.O. Box 17390
Washington, D.C. 20041
(800)278-3135

Price: $25
EIRSP 2015-1-0-0-PDF

Executive Intelligence Review
P.O. Box 17390
Washington, D.C. 20014-0390
1-800-278-3135 (toll-free)

Paper: EIPSP-2015-001-00-000-STD $25
PDF: EIRSP-2015-001-00-000-PDF $25

ISBN (paper): 978-0-943235-26-4
ISBN (PDF): 978-0-943235-27-1

Credits

Editors: Jason Ross, Paul Gallagher
Production: Alan Yue
Printing and Distribution: Robert Bowen
Cover and Title Page design: Alan Yue

Contents

Defend Mankind from the Satanic Climate-Change Swindle

by Helga Zepp-LaRouche

Exactly 70 years after the end of the Nazi dictatorship, preparations are underway— largely unnoticed or misinterpreted by unsuspecting contemporaries—for the establishment of a fascist world government which would exceed Hitler's most audacious dreams. In place of the discredited doctrine of eugenics, which provided the pretense then for the elimination of so-called "inferior races," today it is the swindle of alleged anthropogenic climate change which supplies the argumentation to establish a global eco-dictatorship whose results, and whose declared intention is to eliminate six billion human beings—if it is not stopped.

On November 30-December 11 of this year, the COP21/CMP11 Climate Summit will take place in Paris, also called "Paris 2015." There a binding international convention is supposed to be concluded, obligating every nation in the world to agree to so-called climate goals in order to hold global warming to less than two degrees Celsius. This largest diplomatic conference ever to have taken place in Paris, a mammoth spectacle with about 40,000 participants, is supposed to represent the crowning conclusion to an unprecedented series of dozens of international conferences all during this year on the subject of anthropogenic climate change, aiming to get the agreement of political leaders, industry representatives, union leaders, religious representatives, and social groups of all kinds to this oncoming social contract.

Although this theory, spread with an unprecedented expenditure of propaganda, has by now been swallowed by many credulous people, it is in no way "established science," but rather very "old wine in new wineskins"; namely, the attempt to establish a world government through which to eliminate national sovereignty and thereby the possibility of individuals to participate in government through a representative system. In its place is intended to be a kind of modern feudal oligarchy, in which the club of billionaires and millionaires live in gross luxury while the mass of the population is to be left in backwardness with sharply reduced living standards, lower life expectancies, and reduced cognitive capabilities.

The means to this end is the scare campaign around man-made climate change, which is supposed to induce people voluntarily to do without virtually all the achievements of material and social progress through industrialization. The goal of such an eco-dictatorship is the "great transformation of the world economy" to the exclusive use of so-called renewable energy sources, and thus the decarbonization of the economy, in which both nuclear energy and fossil fuels disappear as rapidly as possible.

The proof offered for anthropogenic climate change consists of pre-fixed computer models, in which the desired result is determined in advance, and segments of historical climate data are selected in such a manner that they appear to demonstrate the effect of so-called greenhouse gases caused by mankind's industrial production and agriculture. But numerous scientists have demonstrated that this game of selecting climate data is entirely willful and staged for this purpose, and that computer-based scenarios are being consciously given out as "scientific" prognoses. There are many studies which show this fakery, and make clear that the man-made portion of the CO_2 concentration in the atmosphere is negligibly low, namely 0.018%; but more importantly, that the connection between CO_2 emissions and climate change is unproven, and thus that the entire argument is based on a spectacular swindle (see Section II of this Special Report).

Driving Energy Technology Down

If one looks at the Earth's climate over the period of millions of years, the changes from warming periods, ice ages, interglacial periods, little ice ages, rewarming

sustainability2009.commerzbank.com

An academic directly deployed by the British Crown since 2004, Hans Joachim Schellnhuber has become the German Merkel government's, and now Pope Francis' climate guru. He asserts that "scientific consensus" puts Earth's population potential at below 1 billion people.

periods after these ice ages, etc. result from cosmic radiation in connection with our Sun's cycles of activity, for which the number of sunspots forms a measure of the Sun's energy production; changes in the characteristics of the Earth's orbit; and the changing position of the Solar System in our galaxy, to name only some of the changing parameters.

What is very well proven, by contrast to anthropogenic climate change, is the connection between the energy-flux density applied in the production process and the number of human beings which can be supported by that production process level (see Section III of this Special Report]. By the intended decarbonization of the world economy combined with simultaneous demonization of nuclear energy, thus reducing society to renewable energy sources, the potential population which can be maintained at these lower energy flux densities is also reduced, and goes roughly to that of the pre-industrial era—a maximum of one billion people.

And just such population reduction is the expressed intention of, for example, Prince Philip, whose unspeakable statement of his wish to be reborn as a deadly virus in order best to support this intention, is notorious. This is also the cynical meaning of Hans Joachim Schellnhuber, head of the Potsdam Institute for Climate Research (PIK) and lately climate advisor to Pope Francis, who—in the course of the fortunately failed Copenhagen Climate Conference of 2009—celebrated as a "triumph of science" and proof of climate change, that planetary equilibrium required a human population of less than one billion.

Behind this lurks the old oligarchic view that the ruling elite is allowed periodically to reduce the population of slaves, helots, or the lower classes which have become too numerous, the way a herd of cattle can be culled as necessary. The idea of mankind connected with this perverse view was exactly described, for example, by Joseph de Maistre in his "Letter to a Russian Nobleman on the Spanish Inquisition." It is the arrogant proposition that only one's own upper class is possessed of essentially God-given privileges, while the mass of people can be terrorized into anxiety and fear, and thus kept under control. The entire history of imperial and colonial periods is a single history of this bestial practice, in which an upper class is viewed as a master race, whose alleged superiority must be defended in every possible way.

A more recent variant of this oligarchical tradition appeared in the form of eugenics, the theory so named by British anthropologist Francis Galton in 1883, according to which it is desirable to strive for the intended purity of this master race by the same kinds of criteria used in the breeding of horses or dogs. At the start of the 20th Century eugenics societies were organized in various European nations and in the United States, which fostered the greatest admiration for the race theory of Adolf Hitler and the National Socialists, and an entire array of whose prominent members and adherents, such as Prescott Bush or Averell Harriman, gave active financial support to the seizure of power by Hitler.

Eugenics Renamed 'Ecology'

After the "successful" application of eugenics in the holocaust operations of Tiergarten 4 and the concentration camps, this bestial method, naturally, was denounced. Julian Huxley, an open sympathizer of eugenics, wrote in 1946 in the official UN Document "UNESCO, Its Purpose and Its Philosophy": "Thus even though it is quite true that any radical eugenic policy will be for many years politically and psychologically impossible, it will be important for UNESCO to see that the eugenic problem is examined with the greatest care, and that the public mind is informed of the issues at stake, so that much that now is unthinkable may at least become thinkable." Huxley launched a campaign to replace the discredited term eugenics with the terms environmental protection, and/or ecology.

Huxley, president of the British Eugenics Society from 1959-62, worked from 1961 onward, together with Prince Philip, on the development of the World Wildlife Fund, WWF, an organization responsible for preventing innumerable infrastructure and development projects around the world, and responsible for a very large share of the misery suffered in countries of the so-called Third World. Prince Philip succeeded, through such fanatical propagandists, in getting the idea of population reduction raised to international political priority; and he pursued above all, the goal of making environmental protection acceptable to the great monotheistic religions, in whose optimistic view of mankind he saw the greatest barrier to his perfidious policies. The Biblical representation of man as the crown of Creation, as Christianity explicitly defined this, had to be replaced by any means, by the conception of human beings as mere caretakers of Nature, not occupying a pre-eminent position but on the contrary, representing a cancer threatening Nature.

As one of many propagators of this brown-green idea, Hans Joachim Schellnhuber distinguished himself, becoming titled as none other than a CBE, Commander of the Order of the British Empire, and founder and director of the Potsdam Institute for Climate Research. Moreover he is, among other things, currently co-chairman of the German government's Scientific Advisory Board on Global Environmental Change (WBGU, Wissenschaftlichen Beirat der Bundesregierung globale Unweltveränderungen), and most recently member of the Pontifical Academy of Sciences. Obscure despite his many titles, Schellnhuber suddenly gained a lamentable fame in the course of the failed Copenhagen Climate Summit in 2009, with his thesis that the carrying capacity of the Earth only allowed a human population of less than one billion.

The Queen Deploys Schellnhuber

Already in 2004 he had been designated by Queen Elizabeth II, together with Sir David King, climate advisor to the British Government and Monarchy, to be sent on a mission to the United States to convince President George W. Bush on anthropogenic climate change. This operation must have far exceeded the bounds which Bush considered acceptable, because he later complained to Tony Blair about it.

Also in 2004, Queen Elizabeth traveled to Berlin to open the German-British Climate Conference, and there granted Schellnhuber the CBE as thanks for his services. The European Climate Foundation, an institution sponsored by hedge funds whose Board of Advisors Chairman was Schellnhuber, thereupon increased its financing of climate activists in Germany from 2007 onwards, while he simultaneously advised the EU Commission on the development of guidelines for CO_2 emissions. As an energy advisor to German Chancellor Angela Merkel, he was presumably responsible for the German exit from nuclear power after the earthquake-tsunami catastrophe of March 11, 2011 in Fukushima.

Interestingly, scarcely one month after the earthquake, on April 7, Schellnhuber's German Government Scientific Advisory Board on Global Environmental Change (WBGU) published a study with the title: "World in Change—Social Contract for a Great Transformation." This was the blunt proposal for a global eco-fascism, a Green world dictatorship in the tradition of Thomas Hobbes, H.G. Wells, and Carl Schmitt, which projected the complete "decarbonization" of the world's energy industry. This means the final elimination of nuclear fission, which is advised against; nuclear fusion, which is claimed to be eventually attainable but too complicated; and the complete abandonment of fossil fuels such as coal, oil, and natural gas by the year 2050.

The study had been six years in preparation and interestingly was designated as a "Master Plan for Social Transformation" by WBGU Chairman Schellnhuber, although it really should be called a master plan for a forced imperial consolidation or even "master plan for the collective suicide of the human race."

For Germany, then, this began its exit as a country in the world community which could contribute something significant, from a scientific standpoint, for the really existential problems of humanity. This began the willful elimination of the potential for scientific discovery of necessary knowledge, because it began to direct human and industrial resources, as well as financial means, into completely delusory fields of technology with lowered energy flux densities. Above all, the intellectual potential of students and researchers was thus absorbed into areas which ultimately represent a dead end in the development of mankind.

The study's methodological approach fully reflected the statistical linear thinking of complex computer models, as they are customarily used by systems analysts, and as we recognized it already, for example, in the Club of Rome: The computer is programmed so that the planned result is produced.

One can only recommend that all citizens read this

Twice in two years, widespread polar ice has diverted or endangered "global warming explorations" in hemispheric mid-Summer. In 2013 the Akademik Shokalskiy became frozen in Antarctic ice in December. Now the Canadian icebreaker Amundsen (above), diverted from global warming research, is back at work since July freeing vessels in Hudson's Bay from record ice.

study for themselves (it can be found at the WGBU's Internet site, www.wbgu.de), and not make the same mistake that was made in Germany about a certain other piece published in 1925—namely, that it was not read thoroughly or taken seriously.

The New Leviathan

What is proposed here *expressis verbis* is a "great transformation" in which production, patterns of consumption, and life styles are all to be fundamentally changed, as happened in both previous fundamental transformations in world history. These two transformations were the transition from hunting and gathering societies to the discovery and spread of agriculture and animal husbandry—the so-called "Neolithic revolution"—and the "industrial revolution," which describes the transition from agrarian to industrial society. This time, however, the transformation is directed backwards, to a "climate-compatible and sustainable world economic order." And this means energy flux densities which, even if the authors naturally do not say so, correspond in reality to the population potential of pre-industrial society, thus roughly 1-2 billion people. It is obvious: If the developing and so-called newly industrialized countries are subject to this eco-dictate, death rates will rise without limit.

In order to be able to create the "contractual basis" for this new sustainable world economic order, the authors bombastically demand a new "world social contract," an idea which is expressly "linked to models in the natural law of early modern societies." They do not expressly mention whether this means a social contract in the sense of Rousseau, which demands the "total alienation of each member of society with all his rights into the whole community," or "the great Leviathan" of Thomas Hobbes, in which the human being transfers rights and powers to the overseer of the state, representing executive, legislative and judicial power in one person who possesses a monopoly of power and cannot be removed from office.

In any case, the new Leviathan, here called "the global governance architecture," and whose highest expression is supposed to be a UN council for sustainable development at the level of the Security Council and reflecting the 21st-Century community of states, is to be the world government representing absolute authority.

Pope Francis Capitulates

The fact that CBE Schellnhuber has gotten his program accepted in the Pontifical Academy of Sciences, raises the most serious questions as to how this was possible. For the most recent encyclical, "Laudato Si'" of Pope Francis, in which anthropogenic climate change is presented as scientifically certain fact, represents a complete break with the view of mankind in the Augustinian tradition of the Catholic Church, and with the encyclicals since Pope Leo XIII. Schellnhuber was one of the three spokesmen who presented the new encyclical on June 18 in Rome.

At a climate conference organized by the Vatican in 2007, the president of the World Federation of Scientists, Antonio Zichichi, rejected the use of computer models as completely unsuitable for long-term climate forecasts on the grounds of the complexity of the problem, and pointed in addition to the multiple influences of the Solar System and the galaxy on the Earth's climate, in opposition to which he characterized the man-made contribution to climate change as absolutely negligible. Several speakers contradicted then-Environment Minister Ed Miliband of Britain, when he claimed that the objectives of the British Government were the same as those of Popes John Paul II and Benedict XVI—rather those Popes were exactly opposed to birth- and population control as proposed by the Brundtland Commission Report and the WWF. And even during the Copenhagen Climate Summit of 2009, the Vatican very clearly attacked the Malthusian tendency of the affair.

With the incorporation of Schellnhuber's ideas into the encyclical and thus the rejection of a serious approach, the Catholic Church has effectively involved itself in a

It took 346 years before Pope John Paul II (inset) formally stated the Catholic Church's error in the case of Galileo, and in 1992 also reflected the modern cosmology of Einstein in his 1992 apology for that error. Now Pope Francis has "effectively involved the Church in a new Galileo case" by capitulating to the global warming/depopulation fraud.

new Galileo case. In that case the Church needed 346 years before Pope John Paul II in 1979, on the occasion of the hundredth anniversary of Albert Einstein's birth, initiated the review of the case, in order then finally to admit the Church's error, after a 13-year trial, in 1992.

In his address to the participants of the full congregation of the Pontifical Academy of Sciences, Pope John Paul II said, *inter alia*:

> From the Galileo affair we can learn a lesson which remains valid in relation to similar situations which occur today and which may occur in the future.
>
> In Galileo's time, to depict the world as lacking an absolute physical reference point was, so to speak, inconceivable. And since the Cosmos, as it was then known, was contained within the Solar System alone, this reference point could only be situated in the earth or in the sun. Today, after Einstein and within the perspective of contemporary cosmology neither of these two reference points has the importance they once had. This observation, it goes without saying, is not directed against the validity of Galileo's position in the debate; it is only meant to show that often, beyond two partial and contrasting perceptions, there exists a wider perception which includes them and goes beyond both of them.

We can only hope that Pope Francis, who otherwise has said very important things about the character of today's system of financial capital—namely that it is a system which violates the Fifth Commandment, "Thou shalt not kill"—will include in his interpretation, our current knowledge of the universe, which encompasses not only our galaxy, whose influence on the climate of this planet is decisive, but billions of galaxies. One could then be confident that he would not support a pseudo-climate policy which thrusts the population potential of the Earth back to one billion.

British Royal Nazis

The attempt of the participants in the "Paris 2015 Conference" to establish binding climate goals whose entire premise is based on a gigantic fraud, which could only be carried out by a global dictatorship—and this in a world in acute danger of destruction in a third, thermonuclear world war, a world whose trans-Atlantic financial system faces an implosion, and in which dozens of millions are already refugees from hunger, war and epidemics—must be decisively defeated in any case. It must go down in history as the last, miserable attempt of the failing British Empire to propagate its inhuman plans, as Prince Philip has proclaimed them *ad nauseam*, before this empire is finally ended.

The most recent revelations on the intensive connections of the House of Windsor to the Nazi regime are not really a surprise for historians. The disclosure of a 17-second family movie in which the 7- or 8-year old Elizabeth—later Queen Elizabeth II—can be seen as she presents the Hitler salute, is only the tip of the iceberg in this regard. In recent weeks hundreds of articles have been circulated, primarily in the British and American press and on the Internet, which throw light on the open admiration of various members of the monarchy and the British nobility for Hitler and the Nazis. The sympathies of Elizabeth's uncle, the later King Edward VIII, who after his abdication became Duke of Windsor, are known. More explosive is the role of Prince Philip, who maintained close connections to high-ranking Nazis through his three sisters, who were all married to leading members of the National Socialist Party and the SS.

The *Times of Israel* published a detailed interview

THE Sun 70

WORLD EXCLUSIVE

Secret 1933 film shows Edward VIII teaching this Nazi salute to the Queen

THEIR ROYAL HEILNESSES

MORE AMAZING PICTURES: PAGES 2, 3, 4, 5, 6 AND 7

Young Princess Elizabeth practiced the Nazi salute in the 1930s in a "palace home movie" which reopened the issue of widespread British nobility support for Hitler and Mussolini at that time. But Prince Philip, with more Nazi "connections" than any other royal, became after World War II perhaps the world's most dogmatic "environmentalist" in demanding the human population be reduced.

with the German-British historian Karina Urbach of the University of London regarding the results of her research on this subject, which she has just published in a book entitled, *Go-Betweens for Hitler* (*Verbindungsleute zu Hitler*). This involves the intensive alliance between broad sections of the British establishment and the Nazis, which played a central role in British geopolitics between the World Wars.

Prince Philip's advisor for religious and climate questions, Martin Palmer, who, in his function as general secretary of the "Alliance for Religions and Environmental Protection," organized a so-called "consciousness summit" in Paris on July 21 in preparation for the December conference, attacked the "anthropocentric salvation doctrine" on that occasion. He meant by this that religions such as Christianity, Judaism and Islam had difficulty understanding that mankind is simply not so important. There must be debate between representatives of these religions, he said, in order to expunge the idea that the human species represents something unique.

'Decarbonization' Is Green Genocide

Here the inhuman ideology comes out, which is just as characteristic of the Conservative Revolution directed against the "ideas of 1789," as it is of the Nazis and the Green movement: The human being is only a higher animal, and therefore human life is not the slightest degree more inviolable than that of animals; one can also reduce the number of human beings if necessary—whether they were the helots in ancient Sparta, or the "useless eaters" of the Nazis, or now the six billion people who must be sacrificed to climate goals. Armin Mohler, the former head of the Siemens Foundation, has already described in his book of the same name, that the Conservative Revolution therefore wants to turn back to the pre-Christian mythology of Gaia, because only the Christian view of mankind brought with it the cultural optimism which made the modern development of the human species possible.

Christianity had this liberating effect for Europe, in any case, and as Nicholas of Cusa formulated it, it was exactly the *vis creativa* of the human being, arising from the human characteristic as *imago viva dei*, the living image of God, which was the basis of the unlimited human perfectibility and of the human identity as the crown of Creation, and not as a higher animal. The same culturally optimistic view is also found in Confucianism in China and was signified in the Vedic writings in India. In the pro-science traditions of these cultures can also be found the reason that both nations, at the Copenhagen Climate Conference in 2009, stood clearly opposed to the climate mafia of anthropogenic climate change, and thus offered backing to the G77 in finally refusing to sign "a suicide pact," as their then-chairman Lumumba Di-Aping of Sudan put it at a press conference.

The recently industrialized and developing countries certainly have all the environmental problems which arise either from forced cheap-labor production or a total lack of development; but this does not mean that they therefore were not in a position to recognize the consequences of the "master plan" for decarbonization of the world economy. It was essentially their populations who belonged to the six billion for whom the carrying capacity of the Earth allegedly does not suffice.

In the improbable case that the Paris 2015 Climate Summit should succeed in adopting binding CO_2 emissions reductions, we can look forward to a world which looks roughly as it would have, had Hitler won the war.

Therefore we must do everything possible to attain a new paradigm in the history of mankind, in which science no longer sells its integrity for money.

How the British Turned Genocide and Race Science "Green"

By Jeffrey Steinberg

At the end of World War II, when the world was still learning of the horrors of the Nazi genocide, and the Nuremberg Tribunals were just barely getting underway, the British Monarchy immediately launched a revival of the very same policies of race science and population genocide that had produced the Nazi euthanasia and the death camps.

Sir Julian Huxley, the grandson of "Darwin's Bulldog" Thomas Huxley, and a leading figure in the British Eugenics Society, used his position as the first Director-General of the United Nations Educational, Scientific and Cultural Organization (UNESCO) to help launch the revival. In a 1946 address, launching the new United Nations agency, he declared, "Even though it is quite true that any radical eugenic policy will be for many years politically and psychologically impossible, it will be important for UNESCO to see that the eugenic problem is examined with the greatest care and that the public mind is informed of the issues at stake so that much that now is unthinkable may at least become thinkable."

While the British Eugenics Society was never disbanded, the revival was carried out under a new banner: ecology and conservation. Just as Hitler's Nazi Party had roots in the radical environmentalist "counterculture" movement of 1920s Germany, the British Crown agents of the immediate post-War years created a series of environmentalist organizations, which would form the basis of the New Eugenics Movement. To this day, those same organizations are the leading promoters, worldwide, of a mass genocide, in the name of "preserving nature."

This was nothing new for the British Crown. Both the Hitler race dogma and population genocide program, and the promotion of preservation of nature over the advancement of mankind, were ideas that were spawned from London in the second half of the Nineteenth Century, through the work of people like Charles Darwin, Sir Thomas Huxley, Sir Francis Galton, Sir Herbert Spencer, and Sir Arthur Tansley, who all led a revival of an extreme form of Malthusian population genocide.

Darwin presented the idea that man had simply evolved from lower species in a strictly quantitative evolution, which he called "natural selection," rejecting outright the qualitatively distinct, non-biological notion of human creative discovery and science itself. Spencer had adapted Darwin's fraud to human existence and developed the Social Darwinist idea of "survival of the fittest." Tansley had first coined the term "ecology," in advancement of the Malthusian revival, placing the preservation of the ecological system over man-enhanced nature. And Darwin's first cousin, Galton, had devised eugenics as a "scientific" approach to culling the human herd of those "unfit" to survive.

In every instance, the common objective of all of these insane, anti-human ideas was to provide a rationale for population reduction, as a means of preserving a system of eternal oligarchical power.

The complete title of Darwin's most famous work, *Origin of Species,* was *On the Origin of Species by Means of Natural Selection, or the Preservation of the Favoured Races in the Struggle for Life* (1859).

The predecessor of this was the 1798 "Essay on the Principle of Population," by Sir Thomas Malthus (1766-1823). Its revival was the basis for the work of Darwin, Spencer, Huxley, Galton and Tansley. Malthus wrote, "All children who are born beyond what would be required to keep up the population to a desired level, must necessarily perish, unless room be made for them by the death of grown persons... Therefore... we should facilitate, instead of foolishly and vainly endeavoring to impede, the operations of nature in producing this mortality; and if we dread the too frequent visitation of the horrid form of famine, we should sedulously encourage the other forms of destruction, which compel nature to use... Instead of recommending cleanliness to the poor, we should encourage contrary habits... but above all we should reprobate specific remedies for ravaging diseases; and restrain those benevolent, but much mistaken men, who have thought they are doing a service to mankind by protecting schemes for the total extirpation of particular disease."

Wikimedia

After Hitler's Nazis discredited eugenics, the Malthusian Sir Julian Huxley created and headed a UN agency, UNESCO, and worked "to make the unthinkable, thinkable again."

Dirty Bertie

A century and a half after Malthus, Lord Bertrand Russell, the intimate of the Huxleys, repeated Malthus's diktat in even more blunt language.

In a 1923 book, *Prospects of Industrial Civilization*, he advanced the doctrine of race supremacy, using the term "international socialism" as a euphemistic alternative to feudalistic oligarchic world dictatorship: "Socialism, especially international socialism, is only possible as a stable system if the population is stationary or nearly so. A slow increase might be coped with by improvements in agricultural methods, but a rapid increase must in the end reduce the whole population to penury... the white population of the world will soon cease to increase. The Asiatic races will be longer, and the negroes still longer, before their birth rate falls sufficiently to make their numbers stable without help of war and pestilence... Until that happens, the benefits aimed at by socialism can only be partially realized, and the less prolific races will have to defend themselves against the more prolific by methods which are disgusting even if they are necessary."

In 1951, in his *The Impact of Science on Society*, which was a discussion of the uses of mass psychology to keep the majority of human beings hopelessly backward and compliant, Russell openly advocated the kind of mass genocide that became the hallmark of the British Royal Consort Prince Philip, as part of his own promotion of "environmentalism." Russell wrote: "Bad times, you may say, are exceptional, and can be dealt with by exceptional methods. This has been more or less true during the honeymoon period of industrialism, but it will not remain true unless the increase of population can be enormously diminished. At present the population of the world is increasing at about 58,000 per diem. War, so far, has had no very great effect on this increase, which continued through each of the world wars... War... has hitherto been disappointing in this respect... but perhaps bacteriological war may prove more effective. If a Black Death could spread throughout the world once in every generation, survivors could procreate freely without making the world too full... The state of affairs might be somewhat unpleasant, but what of it? Really high-minded people are indifferent to happiness, especially other people's."

All of these British high society genocidalists, from the turn-of-the-century British Monarchy onward, were rabid conservationists, preferring unaltered nature to humanity, which they referred to in such terms as "the enemy," "a cancer" and the like.

'New Empire' Ecology

The advancement of the so-called ecology agenda and wildlife protection had another imperial dimension as well. As Britain altered its colonial strategy at the turn of the Twentieth Century, from direct empire to Commonwealth, aiming to establish more indirect control, it became essential to establish firm command over vast swaths of land in Africa. The establishment of game preserves and nature preserves along crucial African borders became a hallmark of the "New Empire" program.

In 1903, the Society for the Preservation of the Wild Fauna of the Empire was established, under the direct control of the British Crown. The model was the "conservancies" that were established by the British Raj over many parts of India to restrict population access.

In 1904, Sir Arthur Tansley founded the British Vegetation Committee. In 1912, the Society for the Promotion of Natural Reserves was formed. The Committee identified 273 areas to be set aside from all human activity. A year later, in 1913, the British Ecology Society was established. Tansley was a central figure in all of these various organizations, and his role as one of the British Crown's chief ecologists continued through and beyond World War II. In the latter phase of his efforts, Tansley worked closely with Sir Julian Huxley and Max Nicholson.

The promotion of conservation and ecology went hand-in-glove with Britain's active promotion of Fascism throughout Europe. In 1931, Huxley and Nicholson created the Political and Economic Planning (PEP) think tank, which produced a series of policy papers actively promoting the corporatist model that had been first put into practice by Benito Mussolini in Italy. PEP closely collaborated with the British Eugenics Society throughout its existence. In 1937, PEP and the BES co-founded the Population Policy Committee, which led, in 1944, to the creation of the Royal Commission on Population. Even throughout the war period, the British Crown was promoting a long-term program of radical population reduction. In 1955, under the joint leadership of Huxley and Nicholson, the PEP published a landmark global profile of human population and natural resources called *World Population and Resources*. It became the guidebook for both the Eugenics/Malthusian apparatus and the so-called "Conservationists" worldwide.

In 1945, Huxley, Tansley, and Nicholson founded the Wild Life Conservation Special Committee, which came to be known as the Huxley Committee, after its chairman. As the result of the Committee's studies on the need for a broad ecology and conservation agenda, the same people shortly founded the British Nature Conservancy, which was to operate directly under the Privy Council, the actual governing body over the British Empire under the Royal Household. Conveniently, from 1945-1952 the secretary of the Privy Council was Max Nicholson. He left that post in 1952, to replace Tansley as head of the Nature Conservancy.

In his official capacity as secretary to the Privy Council, Nicholson had tasked Julian Huxley to lead a study on the conservation of nature in England and Wales, which resulted in a July 1947 report, mapping out areas of the United Kingdom to be set aside as nature preserves. By this time, the Nature Conservancy had been classified as a permanent research arm of the Privy Council, and designated as a scientific body, whose pronouncements were given the authority of scientific certainty.

What was being promoted as a British Crown program to revive eugenics and radical Malthusianism, in the immediate wake of the defeat of Hitler, was "taken global" through Sir Julian Huxley's position as Executive Director of UNESCO. In 1948, Huxley convened a UNESCO-sponsored conference in Fountainebleau, France, where the International Union for the Conservation of Nature (IUCN)[1] was formally launched as an international organization comprised of both governments and non-governmental private organizations. In his keynote speech to the gathering, Huxley declared that "The spread of man must take second place to the conservation of other species."

At this point, the worldwide movement for ecology and nature conservancy was a strictly oligarchical operation—and obviously so. It had no base of popular support, and this remained the case for several decades.

Going 'Popular'

In 1960, Sir Julian Huxley, now 73 years old, made a three-month expedition to Africa, after which he wrote a series of articles in *The Observer*, warning that the newly independent African states could not be trusted to preserve nature and protect the endangered species of the continent. Off of the Huxley expedition, at the initiative of Max Nicholson, the IUCN launched a worldwide popular movement to force the creation of nature preserves and game preserves, under independent international control, throughout the African continent.

Nicholson described the process: "After a memorandum (which I had drafted at Easter in the Cotswolds) had been approved by the IUCN Executive Board, the rest of the preparatory work was done in London by an informal group under my chairmanship between May and September. It culminated in the legal constitution at Zurich of an international charitable foundation called the World Wildlife Fund." The WWF, from its outset, would be housed within the IUCN's Swiss headquarters. The organization was launched at simultaneous press conferences in London and Tanganyika.

Nicholson and Huxley had no trouble getting Royal Consort Prince Philip, already a rabid Malthusian, to

1. Fairfield Osborn, Jr., Nicholson's close friend and a leading eugenicist, had proposed naming the new organization the International Union for the Conservation of Nature and Natural Resources, but the imperial connotations of a global natural resource grab were too flagrant and the name was eventually shortened.

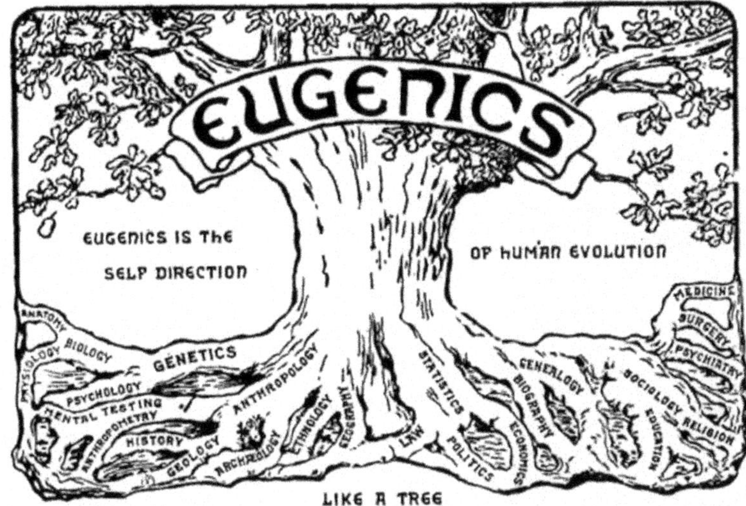

Wikimedia

The British Eugenics Society did not disband after World War II; rather, its leaders around the Crown's Privy Council rapidly created the array of global "environmentalist" and "conservation" institutions and made them powerful through the support of financial oligarchies.

become the head of the British WWF. To avoid the appearance that the organization was purely a creation of the British Crown, the Dutch Royal Consort, Prince Bernhard of the Netherlands, was named as the first international head of the WWF. His own credentials as a long-time card-carrying member of the Nazi Party presented no complications.

With the launching of WWF, as the first effort at a mass social outreach, the founders, particularly Max Nicholson, acknowledged that they were actually out to force a major cultural paradigm shift, away from the notion of human progress, backwards to a dark age concept of man as the "enemy" of nature. In his 1970 book, *The Environmental Revolution: A Guide for the New Masters of the World*, Nicholson wrote of the launching of the WWF:

"We should perhaps look back as far as the Reformation and the Renaissance for a comparable general disintegration of long settled values and patterns through the impact of new outlooks and new ideas... The message of ecology... undermines many recent cherished values and beliefs by a kind of seismic upheaval which is bound to leave in its train heaps of intellectual and ethical rubble. Seismic seems the right word because the emotional force and intensity behind the idea of conservation is as important as its intellectual power."

It is indicative of the true aim of this "seismic change" that Sir Julian Huxley, one of the two genuine architects of the WWF, along with Max Nicholson, was, at the time of WWF's founding, the president of the British Eugenics Society. In 1962, Huxley published an essay under the blunt title "Too Many People," which appeared in a volume titled *Our Crowded Planet: Essays on the Pressures of Population*. Huxley wrote, "Overpopulation is the most serious threat to human happiness and progress in this very critical period in the history of the world. It is not so acute as the threat of atomic warfare, but is graver, since it springs from our own nature... The essential point is that overpopulation is a world problem so serious as to override all other world problems, such as soil erosion, poverty, malnutrition, raw material shortages, illiteracy, even disarmament... If nothing is done about it, in the next hundred years man will cease to have any claims to be the Lord of Creation or the controller of his own destiny, and will have become the cancer of his planet, uselessly devouring its resources and negating his own possibilities in a spate of overmultiplication... for the control of population is, I am quite certain, a prerequisite for any radical improvement in the human lot."

The WWF was launched at the behest of the British Monarchy at a time when cultural optimism was spreading with the election of John F. Kennedy as President of the United States; the launching of the Apollo program, demonstrating man's capacity to conquer new scientific horizons and thoroughly redefine the nature of resources; and the spreading belief that the era of colonialism and empire was coming to an end. Kennedy's launching of the Peace Corps, the prospect of an end to the Cold War with the Soviet Union, initiated in a series of private correspondences between JFK and the Soviet Premier Nikita Khrushchev, and other promising developments, posed a direct threat to the agenda and power of the British Empire.

Mass Mind Control

All of that changed, dramatically, with the assassination of President Kennedy, the ouster of German Chancellor Konrad Adenauer, and the attempted assassinations and eventual overthrow of France's President Charles de Gaulle. With the launching of the U.S. Indochina War, the urban riots, and the assassinations of Robert F. Kennedy and Dr. Martin Luther King, Jr., the

Wikimedia

Zebras in Kruger National Park, South Africa. The park is the size of the state of Massachusetts; in 1902, it was brutally cleared of its non-white inhabitants to turn it into a game preserve for the oligarchy. That policy is being continued today by Prince Philip's conservation and wildlife groups.

optimism of the early 1960s turned into a deep cultural pessimism, particularly among young people in the trans-Atlantic region.

Sir William Sargant, a British military psychiatrist from the Tavistock Institute, who spent over a decade in the United States from the late 1950s to the early 1970s, wrote a 1957 book about the prospects of triggering a mass psychotic breakdown through successive mass social shocks, amplified by the new emerging mass media of television and radio.

In *Battle for the Mind*, which was written while Sargant was an active participant in the U.S. Central Intelligence Agency's MK-Ultra experimentation in mind control, through psychedelic drugs, manipulation of religious superstitions, etc., Sargant wrote:

"Various types of belief can be implanted in many people, after brain function has been sufficiently disturbed by accidentally or deliberately induced fear, anger or excitement. Of the results caused by such disturbances, the most common one is temporarily impaired judgment and heightened suggestibility. Its various group manifestations are sometimes classed under the heading of 'herd instinct,' and appear most spectacularly in wartime, during severe epidemics, and in all similar periods of common danger, which increase anxiety and so individual and mass suggestibility."

Prior to the shock traumas of the 1960s, most Americans and Europeans would have dismissed the radical Malthusian and eugenicist ideas of the WWF as rubbish. Under conditions of shock, those ideas, along with the other manifestations of the drug, rock, sex counterculture, seemed suddenly "normal."

While the WWF was first getting off the ground, a much more public propaganda campaign was launched, to begin spreading the gospel of ecology and conservation. In 1962, Rachel Carson wrote *Silent Spring*, a diatribe against DDT and other agricultural chemicals. This was the first of what would be a string of widely publicized scare-stories, devoid of any scientific foundation, that found an ever more willing mass audience.

In 1968, the Club of Rome was founded as an international agency to popularize the myth that population and economic growth inevitably must fall back, because of limited resources. Its founding document was thus titled, "The Predicament of Mankind," and in 1972, it published the scientifically bogus book, "Limits to Growth," as a mass propaganda item.

In 1970, Prince Bernhard and his close friend Anton Rupert, the South African tobacco magnate, launched the 1001 Club. The purpose of the Club was to generate a guaranteed financial base for the WWF. The secret Club was made up of 1,001 members, whose identity was to be protected. Each member contributed $10,000 per year, establishing a running war chest of $10 million per annum for the WWF's mass propaganda outreach.

Although the membership list in the 1001 Club was to be kept secret, some rosters from the late 1980s were leaked out, and the list of participants revealed a Who's Who of Western and Middle Eastern oligarchs, tycoons and a smattering of outright swindlers and criminals. Thus the 1001 Club included Johannes von Thurn und Taxis of the ancient Venetian oligarchical family, Mossad money launderer Tibor Rosenbaum, arms dealer Adnan Khashoggi, media mogul Conrad Black, and the like. Maj. Louis Mortimer Bloomfield—linked to the assassination of President Kennedy—was a charter member.

Simultaneous to the launching of the 1001 Club, some leading members of the WWF financial arm

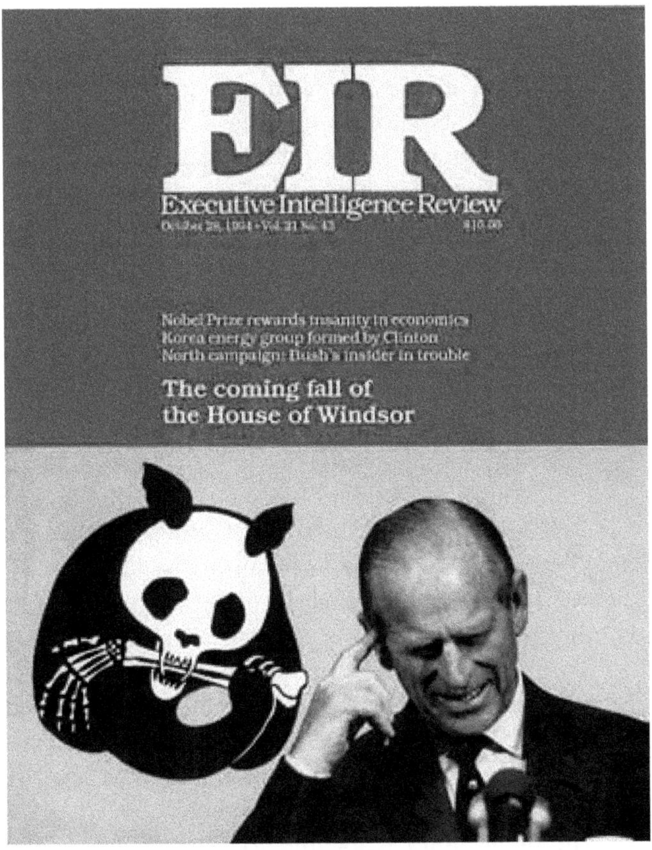

EIR

The most powerful and lavishly funded of the enviro-eugenics organizations, the World Wildlife Fund/WWF, was founded by Prince Philip and Dutch Prince Bernhard, an unreconstructed Hitler Nazi SS member.

launched Earth Day in 1970, an international celebration of the arrival of "ecology" as a new global cause. Canadian Maurice Strong was one of the architects of Earth Day. Two years later, Strong was also a driving figure behind the convening of a United Nations Conference on the Human Environment. At that time Strong was named Executive Director of the newly created United Nations Environment Programme. In effect, Strong inherited the UN mantle from Julian Huxley, who would die three years later.

Closely aligned with the launching of the UNEP, in 1974, the United Nations hosted the third World Population Conference in Bucharest, Romania, with 135 nations participating. One of the key organizers of that conference was the American cultural anthropologist Margaret Mead, an advocate of population control. A featured speaker was John D. Rockefeller, III, whose family had funded the pre-WWII eugenicist "population" movement.

But the event's intended de-population agenda was dramatically blown apart, by the intervention by the Lyndon LaRouche movement, to circulate a $20 billion "Manhattan Project for Fusion Energy Development," presenting a program for R&D and economic advancement, to create effectively inexhaustible power and agro-industrial resources to support a growing human population for centuries. LaRouche associate Helga Zepp, from Germany, presented this growth program, and shocked the Rockefeller plenary, saying that if, instead, the U.N. "environmentalist" program was imposed on the world, the result would be death "100 times worse than Hitler." Conference organizers shut down the session. Zepp then confronted Margaret Mead with the same point on mass death, in front of 200 reporters at the leading press event. (see box).

However, following the conference, Mead peddled the de-population message to the media all the harder. In a signed editorial in the publication *Science*, she declared: "The United Nations Population Conference, which concluded on 31 August in Bucharest, passed by acclamation a World Plan of Action that dramatized the growing global concern for the planet's plight... At Bucharest it was affirmed that continuing, unrestricted worldwide population growth can negate any socio-economic gains and fatally imperil the environment... The earlier extreme views that social and economic justice alone can somehow offset population increase and that the mere provision of contraception can sufficiently reduce population—were defeated...Those governments for which excessive population growth is detrimental to their national purpose are given a target date of 1985 to provide information and methods for implementing these goals."

'Global Warming' Scare Launched

The very next year, Mead organized a conference in Research Triangle Park, North Carolina, where the hoaxes of "global warming" and "climate change" were launched. At the time of both the Bucharest and Research Triangle Park conferences, Mead was president of the American Association for the Advancement of Science (AAAS).

Mead stacked the North Carolina conference with protégés of Paul Ehrlich, the radical Malthusian author of *The Population Bomb*, one of the most rabid propaganda tracts on the need for a total halt in population growth, on the grounds that man posed a threat to the natural ecology of the Earth.

Mead's keynote at North Carolina launched the "global warming" assault on science. "Unless the peoples of the world can begin to understand the immense and long-term consequences of what appear to be small immediate choices—to drill a well, open a road, build a large airplane, make a nuclear test, install a liquid fast breeder reactor, release chemicals which diffuse throughout the atmosphere, or discharge waste in concentrated amounts into the sea—the whole planet may become endangered." Mead demanded a study on "what is presently known about hazards to the atmo-

The Depopulators Challenged: Bucharest, 1974

The LaRouche movement's campaign against the Malthusian elite first gained prominence on the international scene in August 1974, when Helga Zepp and a colleague attended the Third World Population Conference in Bucharest, Romania. By publicly condemning John D. Rockefeller III, the depopulation advocate who had founded the Population Council in 1952, for making proposals that would lead to genocide, the LaRouche representatives blew the conference wide open. "You will be held responsible for your mass-murder policies," they charged, leading to pandemonium.

An indication of precisely how much the exposure hurt the conference organizers was evident after Zepp confronted anthropologist and depopulation advocate Margaret Mead with pushing genocide at a press conference the next day. Mead, who had a habit of carrying a large walking stick, responded by brandishing her stick and chasing Zepp around the room, in a fit of rage.

In fact, the sharp intervention of the LaRouche organizers, along with their presentation of a viable alternative program for fusion-power development, dovetailed with the majority sentiment among the national delegations at the Bucharest conference. This was the first of the international population conferences to bring together country representatives, and the organizers had hoped to get commitments to population control measures, allegedly as a means to further "development."

The agenda for this UN conference represented a "soft-sell," intended to lure Third World nations in particular, into the depopulation, low-technology agenda. As chief genocide spokesman Lester Brown put it: "Either industrial countries will cast Asia adrift, or Western leaders will ask their people to reduce their consumption of livestock in the advanced countries to provide wheat for the Third World."

Rockefeller himself tried to adapt to this outlook. He called for "a more equitable distribution of resources," and a new "concept of economic growth." "We must reorient growth toward human ends, lessen growth of a material kind to improve the lives of people. What is needed is not evaluation on the basis of per capita income, but on social feeling... if famine does occur as a by-product of natural disasters, floods, etc., will people of the industrial countries be willing to cut their food consumption for the starving...?"

Rockefeller's pitch was made even sharper by French zero-Growther Rene Duemont, who insisted that, to liberate the Third World, North Americans must "cut down on the consumption of meat, energy and industrial production immediately."

The pitch didn't work; the conference failed. The "World Population Plan of Action" of the organizers turned into vague platitudes about considering population issues in relation to development goals, and "quality of life."

The very next year [see main article], the anti-population "witch", Mead, organized a conference to change strategy: Malthusianism through "climate change."

The Opposition

In 1982 Helga Zepp herself, now married to Lyndon LaRouche, took a major initiative to organize international forces to defeat the genocide lobby, by proposing the formation of a Club of Life. "The Club of Life views itself as a conscious counterpole to the Club of Rome," she wrote in her Call for Creating a Club of Life, issued January 1 of that year. It shall "be an instrument for those individuals, who, on the eve of a possible collapse of human society, want to intervene with passionate commitmment and political decisiveness in behalf of a new worldwide humanism. ... The Club commits itself to the idea of technological progress and to the value of human beings, which are inseparable from one another."

sphere from man-made interventions, and how scientific knowledge coupled with intelligence social action can protect the peoples of the world from dangerous and preventable interference with the atmosphere upon which all life depends."

Among the Ehrlich-Mead protégés who attended the Research Triangle conference on "The Atmosphere Endangered and Endangering" was John Holdren, currently President Barack Obama's White House Science Advisor. Holdren co-authored a number of books and articles with population fanatic Ehrlich and was an architect of the call for carbon-dioxide caps

EIRNS/Stuart Lewis

Helga Zepp-LaRouche, founder of the Club of Life (here marching in Washington, D.C. in 1983, rallied delegations to reject population control at the Bucharest World Population Conference in 1974, enraging its leaders Margaret Mead and David Rockefeller. Mead unveiled "global warming," a new strategy, one year later.

From October 20-22, 1982, the new institution was founded, with major events in Rome and Wiesbaden, West Germany, plus ten satellite conferences in North and South America, and Paris, France. These conferences drew founding members and speakers from India and Africa, as well as the Americas and Western Europe, all of whom addressed the fight for life in areas of economics, science, and culture.

As Zepp-LaRouche emphasized in her keynote address, "The Club of Life aims at nothing less than to create worldwide a shift toward cultural optimism, as the precondition for the defense of the right to life. We will show, in numerous studies, that the Club of Rome and other organizations of that ilk are charlatans from a scientific standpoint. We will lay bare the motives of those who dare to contest the inviolability of the right to life. But especially we will design concrete programs for development, and bring those to the public, so that everyone can see the solutions that are at hand, if only the political will to implant them is there."

Over the next few years, the Club of Life did exactly what Zepp-LaRouche said. It organized international conferences, rallies, and interventions, and produced literature that exposed the genocidalists, especially the financial institutions and courts who were issuing death sentences to nations, and individuals too weak to defend themselves from the accelerating push for euthanasia. The Club also applied for consultative status at the United Nations, where it would have been a unique voice for development policies.

Thanks to the intervention of zero-growth forces, led by the Swedish representatives, the Club's application was denied.

Today, the thrust of the Club's work has been taken up by the Schiller Institute, founded in 1984 by Helga Zepp-LaRouche on the same principles.

and a concerted plan for population reduction.

In his own summary of the 1975 conference, Holdren warned: "We already have reached the scale of human intervention that rivals the scale of natural processes... Furthermore, many of these forms of intervention will lead to observable adverse effects only after time lags, measured in years, decades, or even centuries. By the time the character of the damage is obvious, remedial action will be difficult or impossible. Some kinds of adverse effects may be practically irreversible."

To deal with the alleged future crisis, the pseudo-scientists at the 1975 conference concluded that they had to launch an international scare campaign, based on the scientifically fraudulent claim that industrialization and other human activities would eventually lead to the destruction of the planet. For example, one of the conference participants, Stephen Schneider, a climate scientist, was outspoken about the scare-mongering involved. He spelled it out to *Discover* magazine some years later, in 1989: "To capture the public imagination, we have to offer up some scary scenarios, make simplified dramatic statements and little mention of any doubts one might have. Each of us as to decide the right balance between being effective and being honest."

All of the essential elements of the global warming scheme were, in fact, put on the table at the 1975 event.

Anthropologist Margaret Mead launched "global warming" as a new population-reduction strategy at a 1975 conference in the United States. Working with her there was John Holdren, now President Barack Obama's Science Advisor; Holdren was a protégé of the discredited "population bomb" inventor Paul Ehrlich.

Implementing the Hoax

What followed was implementation, with the United Nations serving as the venue for intense green propaganda, and ever more coercive pressure for nations to submit to economic destruction in the name of saving the Earth. The International Union for the Conservation of Nature (IUCN) acted officially with the U.N. all the way, under the rubric of "consultative" status, granted under U.N. Resolution 1296, adopted in 1968, under intense IUCN pressure.

In 1982, the U.N. *Charter for Nature* was passed by the U.N. General Assembly. It was prepared by the IUCN. In 1987 the report "Our Common Future" was issued by the World Commission on Environment and Development, mandated in 1983 by U.N. Sec. Gen. Javier Pérez De Cuéllar. The report (known as the "Brundtland Report," after its chairman, Gro Harlem Brundtland) is noteworthy for putting into common parlance the catch-all phrase, *sustainable* development, to extol retrograde modes of power, agriculture, or any other economic practice—modes not actually sustainable at all.

In 1988, the U.N. commissioned the Intergovernmental Panel on Climate Change (IPCC), which became the loudest voice insisting on reducing human numbers and activity, according to the metric of "sustainable development," in order to diminish global warming. From 1990 to 2014, the IPCC has published more than 40 reports on different facets of its "sky-is-falling" message. Teams of authors have churned out thousands of pages under three rubrics: 1) "assessment" of climate change—five sets of four reports per set; 2) eleven "special" reports, e.g., "Safeguarding the Ozone Layer" (2005); and 3) ten "methodology" reports, e.g., on how to measure "wetlands" (2013). Part of the IPCC function has been to demoralize scientists into submission to the green hoaxes.

In 1989, GLOBE International (Global Legislators Organization for a Balanced Environment) was formed —a new world entity aimed at corralling parliamentarians committed to "overseeing the implementation of laws in pursuit of sustainable development." Instigating backers included Tony Blair (UK Prime Minister 1997 to 2007), the UK Foreign & Commonwealth Office, and the London Zoological Society. Today, GLOBE claims legislators in 80 nations.

These initiatives were the run-up to the 1992 Rio Summit, officially the U.N. Conference on Environment and Development, in June, in Rio de Janeiro. The conclave of 172 governments, with 116 heads of state, agreed to the UN Framework Convention on Climate Change (UNFCCC). (A parallel event called "Global Forum" brought together 17,000 participants from NGOs, which went forward as a green strike force.)

Under this new UNFCCC, an annual Conference of the Parties (COP) has been held for 20 years, to push for compliance on reducing greenhouse gas emissions by specified deadlines in the near term. The first confab, COP 1, was held in Berlin in December 1994. At COP 3 in Kyoto, Japan, a text was put forward—known as the "Kyoto Protocol"—for nations to submit to a legally binding agreement, for the goal of collectively reducing global emissions of six greenhouse gases (carbon dioxide, methane and four others) by 5.2% by 2010, compared to 1990. (This represents a cut of over 25%, relative to the trend of expected levels of emissions.) Many nations balked. A series of "commitment periods" was begun, in an attempt to keep the process going, starting with 2005-2012, and then 2012 to 2020 (known as the Doha Amendment period), which was modified at COP20 in Lima, Peru in December 2014. As of July 2015, 36 nations have signed on. Now COP21 is set for December 2015, in Paris, amidst fierce pressure on nations to finally submit en masse.

The continuing mandate, with or without the nicety of treaties, is for nations to devise and implement their own green grab-bag of so-called Earth-saving actions of "for's and against's": for "renewable energy" (biomass, solar, wind); for "sustainable" agriculture and industry; against chemicals, against pollution, against fossil fuels, against water "over-use," and so on. The intent: against people.

'The Enemy Is Humanity'

The intended result of this process is to kill people. The toll of death and deprivation is measurable, under the various green mandates for curbing necessary activity across the different sectors of the economy—power, water, farming, industry, transportation, and even space.

POLLUTION. One of the foremost scare stories involving protecting Mother Earth from man-made pollution and noxious modern chemicals, is that DDT is dangerous. In 1972, its use was banned in the U.S., as a result of green fascist intervention in Washington, D.C., and DDT usage internationally was drastically diminished over succeeding decades. The result: some 70 million needless deaths from malaria worldwide—mostly in Africa—over the period 1973 to 2014. At present, there are over 200 million needless cases of malaria each year, and over 500,000 deaths. An estimated 3.3 billion people are at risk from malaria today, according to the latest World Health Organization evaluation.

RENEWABLE FUELS. Another deadly green hoax, is that bio-mass fuels—ethanol, gasohol, bio-diesel—are desirable as "renewables." This means, in fact, that vast areas of land are under cultivation—from U.S. corn fields, to Brazilian cane, to Southeast Asian palm groves—to produce fuels to go up in smoke.

Labor, machinery, seed and chemical inputs are likewise sucked into the process of degradation of agriculture. In 2005, the U.S. passed a "Renewable Fuel Standard" law mandating an annual volume of U.S. biofuel production, used in gasoline (corn ethanol), which over the last decade, has accordingly expanded internationally. The loss of food is immense. As of 2010, a third of the U.S. corn harvest—which itself accounts for more than a third of world corn production—went to ethanol. This quantity of corn would have had the potential to feed 560 million people, had it not been burned.

There are many other blatant examples. Thus, we are seeing the green goal of depopulation in action.

There could be no more explicit statement of this goal, than that by the Club of Rome in its 1991 document, *The First Global Revolution*: "In searching for a new enemy to unite us, we came up with the idea that pollution, the threat of global warming, water shortages, famine and the like would fit the bill...But in designating them as the enemy, we fall into the trap of mistaking symptoms for causes. All these dangers are caused by human intervention and it is only through changed attitudes and behavior that they can be overcome. The real enemy, then, is humanity itself."

British Crown's Depopulation Pope: CBE Hans Joachim Schellnhuber

The "climate expert" who presented to the world the Catholic Pope's capitulation to the global warming swindle, Hans Joachim Schellnhuber, Commander of the Order of the British Empire (CBE), has been directly deployed by the British Crown since at least 2004 on missions to bring governments into line on "climate and environmental protection." He is also a member of the Club of Rome, which burst upon the world 45 years ago with a systems-analysis computer model of the future of the human species—*Limits to Growth*—which was proven to be, and later admitted to be, a fraud based on a deliberate "deletion" of human technological progress.

In the rush of fame which accompanied Schellnhuber's Mephistophelian role in Pope Francis' encyclical *Laudato Si'*, he has emphasized that he took a hard line among other Papal advisors regarding the document: It had not only to accept global warming, but attribute it *entirely* to mankind's activities. On the other hand, Schellnhuber has tried hard to deny that he brought the demand for population reduction into the Vatican; but he is on the record. At the 2009 Copenhagen Climate Summit, for which he organized on behalf of Prince Charles of Britain, Schellnhuber claimed in his public presentation that the Earth's "carrying capacity" would allow a human population of only about 1 billion.

For a mathematical physicist unknown to the public until very recently, Schellnhuber has a wide variety of titles, including those above. He is a member of the global-warming "authority," the Intergovernmental Panel on Climate Change (IPCC). He was the German government's Chief Advisor on Climate during Germany's 2007 EU Council Presidency; he is also an Advisory Board member at Deutsche Bank. He directs the German government's Advisory Council on Global Climate Change, which in turn is directing Germany's suicidal "exit from nuclear power." He is recently a member of the Vatican Academy of Sciences.

After having founded the Potsdam Institute on Climate (PIK), Schellnhuber was brought to the United Kingdom in 2002, to assume the post of Research Director at the Tyndall Centre for Climate Change Research in Norwich, a branch of Oxford University's Tyndall Center. He was also brought on to the Oxford University Physics Department and the Environmental Change Institute. He was at the "authoritative" East Anglia Climatic Research Unit when it was found that global warming researchers there were exaggerating their data for purposes of influencing energy policy. Schellnhuber organized a Nobel Prize holders' "Conference on Global Sustainability" in 2011, and arrogantly commented then about the East Anglia scandal, "When one has become a Nobel Prize winner . . . one is permitted to speak about moral standards, for then, when one has 'been knighted,' so to speak, one is raised above any doubt. . ." video text here

A Series of Royal Missions

Schellnhuber is one of a team of royal "climate advisors" deployed globally by the Crown, including Prince Philip's advisors Martin Palmer and Sir David Attenborough. In early 2004, Queen Elizabeth II considered Professor Schellnhuber as the best man for a sensitive operation to pressure President George W. Bush into agreeing to the anthropogenic climate-change swindle. Schellnhuber traveled to Washington, D.C. along with Prime Minister Tony Blair's top science advisor, Sir David King, who is now the British Crown's Special Representative for Climate Change, appointed by the Foreign and Commonwealth Office in September 2013. The Bush White House reportedly formally complained to British Prime Minister Blair about this mission.

Also in 2004, the Queen traveled to Berlin to open a British-Germany conference on environmental protection and it was there that she dubbed Schellnhuber a

Commander of the Order of the British Empire.

In 2005, Blair turned to Schellnhuber to organize a conference on "Avoiding Dangerous Climate Change," at the G8 summit in Gleneagles, Scotland.

With Professor Schellnhuber as chairman of the advisory board, the European Climate Foundation (ECF), from 2007 on, generously funded German "climate activists" while at the same time, Schellnhuber was working with the EU Commission on guidelines for the reduction of CO2 emissions.

In 2009, Schellnhuber, in close collaboration with Prince Charles, coordinated preparations for the UN Copenhagen Climate Conference (COP15). Preparations included another mission to Washington, this time to personally press the Obama Administration on the urgency of the monarchy's global "decarbonization" intent. Schellnhuber's work here was easy: Obama's Science Advisor was and is depopulation champion John Holdren, a long-time associate and collaborator of Schellnhuber and a Paul Ehrlich follower who worked with Margaret Mead on the first "global warming" conference in 1975. (Obama himself has more recently confessed his doting admiration for anti-human population guru Sir David Attenborough's work.) The Copenhagen conference nonetheless failed, after representatives of developing and emerging countries—and the Vatican—realized that the intention behind the climate question was massive population reduction.

www.pnas.org

The Pope's adoption of the "global warming" agenda—including the idea of mankind as pollution on the Earth—is a disastrous event for humanity, and a victory for the British Royal Family, acting through this man: Hans Joachim Schellnhuber.

Master Plan for Feudal Oligarchy

Schellnhuber's most successful Crown deployment, prior to the conquest of Pope Francis, was his role as German Chancellor Angela Merkel's energy advisor and head of the German Government Advisory Council on Global Change (WGBU). Shellnhuber bears the main responsibility for inducing Merkel to make the climate-change question the top agenda item during Germany's presidency of the EU in 2007—something which not only wrecked Germany as an industrial nation, but also seriously compromised Merkel's personal integrity as a scientist.

And in 2011, in his capacity as chairman of the WBGU, Shellnhuber presented a master plan for a "World in Transition: A Social Contract for a Great Transformation," a proposal for establishing a worldwide eco-fascist order, published March 17, 2011 by the WGBU.

Here Schellnhuber said, "The requisite decarbonisation of energy systems means that the pressure is on to act, not just in the industrialised countries, but also in the dynamically growing newly industrialising and developing countries. Even the poorer developing countries must veer towards a low emission development path in the medium term. *The era of fossil energy carrier reliant economic growth must be brought to an end.*" [emphasis added]

A fundamental overhaul of the UN to make it a world environmentalist government did not exceed his "knightly" ambition:

> Considering the scale of the described challenges of the transformation, the WBGU believes that there are plenty of arguments for an even more radical approach that would go beyond the existing UN architecture, a fundamental restructuring of the organisation. Currently, this does not seem feasible in political terms, as it would need a political leadership that is guided by a profound realisation of vital global necessities, for example, in the UN Security

Council as well as other industrialised and newly industrialising countries.

If this were the case, a reform should start with a review of the UN Charter, and aim for a completely restructured United Nations organisation. Its purpose would be to take the planetary guard rails into account as a guiding principle that governs UN actions, and the pursuit of which would guarantee protection of climate and environment as much as peace, security and development.

Orders were issued to the BRICS nations and to other nations in Asia, Africa and South America to give up their nuclear programs:

> Several countries are currently planning to increase their use of nuclear energy. The WBGU urgently advises against this, above all because of the not negligible risk of serious damages, the still unresolved issues concerning final storage, and the danger of uncontrolled proliferation. Existing plants should be replaced by sustainable energy technologies as soon as possible, and, in the case of evident safety deficiencies, be closed down immediately. However, the phase out of nuclear energy must not be compensated by renewed or intensified brown or black coal-based energy generation.

And for his Nobel Prize holders' conference "on global sustainability" that year, Schellnhuber wrote in a statement, "Unsustainable production, consumption, and population growth endanger the carrying capacity of the planet to sustain human activity." And under the subhead, "Reducing the Pollution of Human Beings," this Schellnhuber document continued, "Consumption, inefficient use of raw materials, and inappropriate technologies are the main reasons for the growing human burden on the planet. Population growth must be addressed."

Seeing Promethean Fire as Pollution

On May 3 of this year, in an interview in the *Frankfurter Allgemeine Zeitung*, Schellnhuber broadened the denunciation to "fire" in general, echoing the rejection of Promethean fire in the encyclical *Laudato Si'* which he co-wrote for Pope Francis. "In the age of fire, mankind has grown to a certain planetary power. . ." he said. "And thus we are steering on in complete ignorance of the firewalls of the planetary system. Is there an alternative course? There are many! But all require, not reform, but rather the early defeat of the fossil-nuclear complex."

Schellnhuber then proposed the remaking of representative democracy: The propagation of international environmental protection legislation through the UN; and the reservation of 5-10% of the seats in national parliaments for appointed "ombudsmen for the rights of future generations." These ombudmen, he suggested, would organize referenda against the energy policies of the "fossil-nuclear complex."

These statements characterizing the human species as planetary pollution, and population growth as destroying the planet, indicate the reason for Hans-Joachim Schellnhuber's great usefulness for the British oligarchy, his positions at the World Bank, Deutsche Bank, on international committees, and his imposition on Chancellor Merkel's government and the Vatican by the British Crown.

The Encyclical from Hell

by Paul Gallagher

Anyone who reads the encyclical written by Commander of the Order of the British Empire John Schellnhuber for issuance by Pope Francis, cannot escape its call for the destruction of mankind—that sinful and violent race made from the mere soil of the creator "Mother Earth."

Pope Francis presumably does not want to wipe out most of the human species. But the British Royal Family does—publicly so—and the Pope has capitulated to the leading Satanic forces on Earth. The Encyclical *Laudato Si'* is a horrible corruption of the Catholic Church and of Christianity. It is also an assault against science, technological progress, and the idea of human beings as co-creators with the Creator.

The fact that the Pope of 1.2 billion Catholics—the Vatican which has blocked international "climate conferences" from issuing the British royals' Malthusian global edicts—has been roped into issuing and promoting *Laudato Si'*, represents a threat to human civilization of the most serious nature.

The controlling author of the Encyclical was Hans Joachim "John" Schellnhuber of Oxford, who states that the maximum number of human beings which can be sustained by "Mother Earth" is "less than 1 billion." He is momentarily and violently trying to deny these statements, but they were made at international climate conferences and reported in major press.

The British royals, and their other leading anti-science agents such as Martin Palmer and Sir David Attenborough, shamelessly state that the human race is a pollution of Mother Earth—its growth is the root of all evils and problems, according to Sir David—and should be leveled, by any means necessary, to "less than 1 billion" in number. *Laudato Si'* author Schellnhuber has been a personal agent deployed by and with Queen Elizabeth and Prince Charles since at least 2004, to demand that major governments agree to "decarbonize" and scrap modern industry.

Prometheus Again Bound

From the opening words of *Laudato Si'*, this Encyclical stands opposed to all others dealing with social matters by the Popes since Leo XIII. Whereas those encyclicals always put the human being "in the center" as most beloved of the Creator, this one pictures mankind as the great polluter, if not pollution itself.

Pollution, moreover, of a different creator, called "Mother Earth."

> Praise be to you, my Lord, through our Sister, Mother Earth, who sustains and governs us, and who produces various fruit with coloured flowers and herbs," the Encyclical opens [as translated to English on the site of the Holy See].
>
> 2. This sister now cries out to us because of the harm we have inflicted on her by our irresponsible use and abuse of the goods with which God has endowed her. We have come to see ourselves as her lords and masters [having been given "dominion" over her, is a better translation of the original into English—ed.], entitled to plunder her at will. The violence present in our hearts, wounded by sin, is also reflected in the symptoms of sickness evident in the soil, in the water, in the air and in all forms of life. This is why the Earth herself, burdened and laid waste, is among the most abandoned and maltreated of our poor; she 'groans in travail' (Rom 8:22). We have forgotten that we ourselves are dust of the earth (cf. Gen 2:7); our very bodies are made up of her elements, we breathe her air and we receive life and refreshment from her waters.

The worship of Mother Earth as creator, is paganism, including its Satanist forms. This rejects both the scientific view of mankind's activity, and the Christian one—*Genesis* itself.

"Inasmuch as we all generate small ecological damage, we are called to acknowledge our contribution, smaller or greater, to the disfigurement and destruction of creation."

Did the ancient Greeks disfigure and destroy the shore on which they built Athens, or the sea on which they sailed? Did Kepler disfigure and destroy the Solar System by discovering God's design of it? Astronauts by exploring it? Do our spacecraft destroy the Earth by mapping and measuring it? Did oil disfigure the smoky wood-burning society which preceded it, or the discoverers of nuclear isotopes disfigure and destroy medical patients? How many of those "flowers and fruits" were created in the biosphere by the human species?

Despite covering itself in passing quotes from every

conceivable previous Papal document, this one is their opposite. Compare what Schellnhuber et al. quote from Saint John Paul II's *Redemptor Hominis*:

> Authentic human development has a moral character. It presumes full respect for the human person, but it must also be concerned for the world around us and take into account the nature of each being and of its mutual connection in an ordered system.[8] Accordingly, our human ability to transform reality must proceed in line with God's original gift of all that is;

NASA

Pollution? Are these Earth-mapping satellites "contributing a small amount of pollution every day," for which their guilty builders should apologize to Mother Earth, as the encyclical Laudato Si' claims? Is the human development shown in light below, "pollution" burdening Mother Earth? No previous papal encyclical has claimed so.

with what Schellnhuber et al. wrote for Pope Francis in *Laudato Si'*:

> We must be grateful for the praiseworthy efforts being made by scientists and engineers dedicated to finding solutions to *man-made* problems [emphasis added]. But a sober look at our world shows that the degree of human intervention is actually making our earth less rich and beautiful, ever more limited and grey, even as technological advances and consumer goods continue to abound limitlessly. We seem to think that we can substitute an irreplaceable and irretrievable beauty with something which we have created ourselves.

The Encyclical plods through the most superficial two- to three-paragraph glosses on forms of "pollution"; almost appealing to the sub-teenaged "pollution—eeuuw, gross!" without attempting any scientific or engineering depth, possible advances, or possible solutions.

Some might try to excuse this, reciting, "The Pope is not an economist." But *Laudato Si'* is Malthusian economics, of the most evil kind. It would again take from mankind the Promethean fire of technology, and push humanity down to the wretched state from which Prometheus rescued it.

The encyclical declares Promethean foresight "wrong."

> An inadequate presentation of Christian anthropology gave rise to a wrong understanding of the relationship between human beings and the world. Often, what was handed on was a Promethean vision of mastery over the world....

The paragraph dismisses "the human being in the center"—anthropocentrism is "misguided."

Most criminally, it declares that progress is a "myth," and it effectively denies that scientific and technological progress can uplift the poor, making this British encyclical from Hell a direct attack on the developing nations first of all.

Resistance

Through this Encyclical, the British Royals have laid claim to control of the Roman Catholic Church with its 1.2 billion adherents.

They showed off their control of the U.S. President with a shameless "BBC America" program June 28 in which Obama brought genocidalist David Attenborough to the Oval Office, played BBC interviewer for him, lavishly praised Attenborough, and agreed to his statements that population growth is the world's most serious problem.

Thus, the royals can now give the "go" signal to their puppet Obama, to solve the overpopulation problem within a few hours by triggering his confrontations with China and Russia into actual thermonuclear war.

If you believe in the future of our unique human species—on this planet and in the Solar System and the galaxy—you must mobilize yourself now to save humanity from the threat represented by this encyclical.

Prince Philip: Founding Father of The Environmentalist Movement

by Alicia Cerretani

> *"In the event I am reborn, I would like to return as a deadly virus, in order to contribute something to solve overpopulation."*
>
> – Prince Philip, 1988

If there was one man, without whose championing of the modern day environmentalist movement it would not exist today, it is HRH Prince Philip. Most people may find it hard to believe that a royal, a high-ranking member of the world's most powerful financial and military empire, and who has enjoyed the most lavish lifestyle of any human being on the planet, has played such a crucial role in launching the environmentalist and conservation movements today. Then again, most people believe the environmentalist movement is about saving the environment.

University of Salford Press Office

The Prince who would cull the world's human population like cattle, or kill them with disease

Born Prince Philip of Denmark and Greece on June 10, 1921, during a period of great geopolitical tumult for Europe and the British Empire, Philip would be raised, as were all the European elite, to make sure the interests of the European oligarchic establishment survived anything, including two world wars.[1]

It is through the ongoing life of Prince Philip that we see the same fascist ideology of eugenics, which propelled Hitler into power, evolve into a new form of fascism, "environmentalism." This new form of fascism, as envisioned by Prince Philip, is, in reality, a global concentration camp used to starve the world's population of resources under the pretense of conserving them to protect the environment, forcing the majority of the world's population to live off of less than what is required to survive.

Nazi Upbringing

Philip was raised to believe in the "superior race." Eugenics, a scientific construct of the British Empire, was commonly taught, and was used as justification for colonial powers' imperial conquests. Beginning in 1933, Philip was educated on "race science" and a love of the great outdoors at Kurt Hahn's Schloss Salem school in Germany and later in Scotland.

In these years, perhaps due more to a disgust for the "lesser races," Philip is said to have cultivated a fascination of the "rules" of the natural world. In the preface to his 1989 book, Down to Earth, Philip says,

> *"I don't claim to have any special interest in natural history, but as a boy I was made aware of the annual fluctuations in the number of game animals and the need to adjust the 'cull' to the size of the surplus population."*

As an adolescent and young man, an important influence in Philip's life was his uncle Lord Mountbatten (formerly Lord Battenberg until he "Anglicized" his name after WWI). It was Mountbatten who brokered the marriage between Philip and then-Princess Elizabeth in 1947, securing Philip's place in the House of Windsor, as consort to the heir apparent to the British throne.

During the war, while serving in the British Navy, Lord Mountbatten and his sister Louise, Philip's aunt,

1. "The Immorality of the House of Windsor," Scott Thompson November 28, 1997

Philip's royal influence was pushed by British Viceroy in India Lord Mountbatten, shown here with Lady Mountbatten talking to Gandhi. Lord Mountbatten oversaw the last of the British Empire's artificially created famines in India.

crown princess of pro-Nazi Sweden, operated as the channels of communication between the British royals and their pro-Hitler family in Germany. The release of these communications is still hotly contested; they have remained classified by orders of the Queen to this day.

The other highly disturbing factor of Prince Philip's relationship to Lord Mountbatten, is what must have been Philip's exposure, early and often, to the known pedophile habits of British lords and dukes. The long history of abuses perpetrated by "esteemed" British elites including Lord Mountbatten, close family friend Jimmy Savile and Philip's son Prince Andrew today, reflect a culture of rampant degeneracy, an environment which the young prince was raised as to view as "normal."

More insight into what passed as "normal" or expected of Philip and his siblings can be gleaned from the marriages of his four older sisters, who, within a year, from 1931 to 1932, each married into the pro-Nazi, German-Austrian aristocracy, further tightening the alliance among some of Europe's most fascist elite families. His oldest sister, Margarita, married Gottfried von Hohenlohe-Langenburg, a Czech-Austrian prince and great-grandson of England's Queen Victoria; Theodora married Berthold, the Margrave of Baden; Cecilia married Georg Donatus, Grand Duke of Hesse, also a great-grandson of Queen Victoria, and Sophie married Prince Christoph of Hesse, chief of the Forschungsamt, a secret Nazi electronic eavesdropping operation run by Herman Goering. Christoph was also Standartenführer, or colonel of the SS on Heinrich Himmler's personal staff.

At 18, Philip, the youngest of his siblings, began to court a 13 year old Elizabeth in 1939. Just three years earlier, in 1936, she had become heir apparent when her father assumed the throne as King George VI. Of course, having a Nazi pedigree among the English oligarchy wasn't anything out of the ordinary, and Elizabeth's family was no exception. Her father ascended the throne in 1936 when her uncle, King Edward VIII, was forced to abdicate after only one year as King, due to his Nazi loyalties.

'Conservation': The Empire's Strategy for the 21st Century

As discussed elsewhere in this report, throughout the WWII years, the British Empire/Commonwealth needed to maintain its global financial hegemony without having the direct dominion status it had enjoyed before. Not only had a significant amount of the empire been lost, there was now a post-war global development framework to contend with, one set into motion by their American allies, specifically FDR.

How could the British Crown and the rest of the European oligarchy counter the rising power of the U.S. and the national independence and global development movement sweeping the planet? Get people to believe that development is a bad thing, specifically the development of the third world.

It was in these post-war years that the decision was made to mobilize the full arsenal of the Crown to create a worldwide movement promoting conservation and protecting the natural world, and Prince Philip was chosen to become its leading spokesman.

> *"We talk about over- and underdeveloped countries; I think a more exact division might be between underdeveloped and overpopulated. The more people there are, the more industry and the more waste and the more sewage there is, and therefore the more pollution."*
>
> –Prince Philip, Address to Edinburgh University Union, November 24, 1969

In 1961 Prince Bernhard of the Netherlands, Prince Philip, and Sir Julian Huxley founded the World Wildlife Fund, an organization which would become the largest conservation organization in the world. Because the British were then infamous for their imperial meddling, it was decided that Prince Bernhard would become the first president of the WWF, instead of Philip. The WWF set out, with the full backing of the British Empire, to push the conservation campaign globally.

In 1966, Prince Philip established the Australian Conservation Foundation (ACF), Australia's first environmental organization, which also would become Australia's most prominent environmental organization to this day. In 1970 Philip authored a full-page feature in the *Melbourne Herald*, titled "Wildlife Crisis: Every Life Form Is in Danger". Under the subhead "Plague of People," Philip declared: *"The phenomenon now widely described as the population explosion means that the human race has reached plague proportions."*[2]

Prince Philip, Princess Elizabeth, and Prime Minister Louis St. Laurent, circa 1951

Philip served as President of the Australian Conservation Foundation from 1971 to 1976, intervening directly into the affairs of the government. Philip wanted to make an example out of Australia: Conservation, not development, was the post-war strategy of the Crown, and the Commonwealth had better get on board.

> *I was in Sri Lanka recently, where a United Nations project set out in the late 1940s to eradicate malaria. It's an island and it was therefore possible to destroy the mosquito carrying the disease. What people didn't realize was that malaria was actually controlling the growth of the population. The consequence was that within about 20 years the population doubled. Now they've got to find something for all those people to do and some way to feed them.*
>
> *Human population growth is probably the single most serious long-term threat to survival. We're in for a major disaster if it isn't curbed--not just for the natural world, but for the human world. The more people there are, the more resources they'll consume, the more pollution they'll create, the more fighting they will do. We have no option. If it isn't controlled voluntarily, it will be controlled involuntarily by an increase in disease, starvation and war.*
>
> –Prince Philip, Interview with People magazine, December 1981

And so it began. The British Commonwealth soon contained the largest total acreage of "protected" land on the planet.[3] Sounds responsible, doesn't it? These are also the poorest nations, and least sovereign governments in the world. With the Crown sitting on these 'nations' natural resources, they have zero freedom to develop their internal economies and labor force.

Throughout the 1980s, the WWF began to take over huge swaths of land in Africa. Julian Huxley, co-founder of the WWF, after having taken a safari throughout the continent in 1960, asserted that African cultures couldn't be trusted to take care of their own land. Now, the WWF could do that for them. By the mid 1990s, the WWF had gained control of over 8% of the African continent, almost 2,000,000 square kilometers, of "protected" land.

A major ideological counter to Prince Philip throughout the 20th century, and his I'd-like-to-come-back-as-a-deadly-virus attitude toward his fellow man, has been the Catholic Church. As a champion of the dignity of man and empowering of the poor, the Church, representing some of the poorest people on the planet, has insisted that man's creativity is his own best resource, the antithesis of Prince Philip's raison d'etre.

In 1986 at the 25th anniversary celebration of the founding of the WWF, Philip set his sights on recruiting the major religions of the world to the religion of conservation, and founded the "WWF Religion and Con-

2. "Heil Philip!" CEC aust.com.au, 2011

3. http://data.worldbank.org/indicator/ER.LND.PTLD.ZS

ARC/Katia Marsh

Prince Philip and his long-time advisor Martin Palmer have concentrated for 30 years on trying to win over the leaders of the world's major religions to the worship of Nature instead of God, and the elimination of the idea of mankind's dominion over the Earth.

servation Network." It was here that Philip and his protege and ARC co-founder, Martin Palmer, laid the groundwork to eventually infiltrate the Catholic Church.

> *It is now apparent that the ecological pragmatism of the so-called pagan religions, such as that of the American Indians, the Polynesians, and the Australian Aborigines, was a great deal more realistic in terms of conservation ethics than the more intellectual monotheistic philosophies of the revealed religions.*
>
> –Prince Philip, "Caring for Creation" conference, Washington, D.C., May 18, 1990

In 1992, Martin Palmer published a book titled *Coming of Age: An Exploration of Christianity and the New Age*, in which he states that Christianity was guilty of "deification of humanity and its products, science and industry."

Three years later, in 1995, at a conference at Windsor Castle, Philip and Palmer founded the Alliance of Religions and Conservation (ARC), an organization set up to infiltrate the world's major faiths and recruit them to make a religious cause out of global warming and "protecting" the natural environment. Twenty years later, the head of the Catholic Church, Pope Francis, would publish the *Laudato Si'* encyclical, asserting some of the most anti-human, anti-scientific regurgitations from Philip and his decades-long conservation campaign.

For someone promoting less people and less development in the world, Prince Philip, Royal Consort to the Queen, has certainly lived a long, luxurious life of pushing this Nazi-inspired campaign on the rest of the world.

> *Everyone thinks it's to do with not enough food, but it's really that demand is too great—too many people. Basically, it's a little embarrassing for everybody. No one quite knows how to handle it. Nobody wants their family life to be interfered with by the government.*
>
> –Prince Philip, interview with Britain'sTV channel ITV1 on the world food crisis, 2008

Instead of canceling the humanitarian and environmental crisis that is the British Monarchy, the world's population has instead, thanks to the endless resources of the British Monarchy, been led to believe in one of the most hysterical scientific frauds ever perpetrated on mankind.

Today's green movement vilifies the very scientific and technological progress that makes mankind a unique and powerful geological force on the planet. Not only are the effects of this ideological warfare immoral, they are scientifically inaccurate, as we have outlined in this report.

There is no place in the 21st century for Philip, the monarchy, their view of man, or their so-called "environmentalism." It is time these 20th century ideas were put to rest. The next generation of leaders tasked with bringing nations together around mutually beneficial development, what Chinese president Xi Jinping calls "win-win" cooperation, have no use for them.

It appears that according to the "natural world," it is time the old British Monarchy finally went extinct, making way for higher, more complex, intelligent forms of life.

Develop the Ultimate Resource—the Mind; Reject Environmentalist Baby-Killers

Author and former long-time environmentalist Paul Driessen was interviewed Aug. 12 by Jason Ross for LaRouchePAC.

Ross:: Hi, I'm Jason Ross here with LaRouchePAC, sitting down for an interview with Paul Driessen, the author of *Eco Imperialism: Green Power, Black Death* and a Senior Policy Adviser for the Committee For A Constructive Tomorrow (CFACT), an institution devoted to reversing the excesses and errors of environmental regulation. Now, Paul, this hasn't always been your relationship to the environmentalist movement. Could you tell us a bit about yourself?

Driessen:: To me, my relationship is much like President Reagan said about his to the Democratic Party: I didn't leave the environmental movement—the environmental movement left me. And the gist of it is, we started this movement back in the '60s, when I was still in college. I was part of that initiative. We had major pollution problems, water and air quality, all kinds of issues. And over the years, because we developed new laws, new regulations, new attitudes, new policies, a whole new mindset about the environment, we took care of those problems.

We met our goals and went way beyond them. For example, pollution levels from the early '70s for the main, criteria pollutants, NOx (nitrous oxides) and SOx (sulphur oxides) and all those, are down at least 72%. And power plants emit maybe a tenth of what they used to send out into the environment. Cars are about 95% cleaner than they were when we started all this.

But over the years, as we met those goals and achieved those huge victories, the more radical elements of the environmental movement took over. They had always been there, but they were relegated to the back burner because we were focusing on the real, serious, legitimate problems. So as they moved forward and took the ascendancy, they started pushing views

EIRNS/Alicia Cerretani

Paul Driessen: "To master resources, energy, affordable, reliable, abundant energy, the ultimate resource is our creative minds, and our ability to find new ways to do things, new resources."

that Patrick Moore, co-founder of Greenpeace, and I and lot of others view, as being anti-science, anti-technology, anti-reality, anti-evidence, and anti-people.

So that's when I took my leave. I just decided that the environmentalists were essentially battling the things I believed in. I think we *need* technologies to move us forward, to improve people's living standards and well-being, and reduce deaths. And we've done that here in *this* country. But there are billions of people in the rest of the world, who still need to have the technologies, the affordable, reliable, carbon-based energy, that we have used to raise our living standards, our health, and our well-being way beyond anything imaginable even a hundred or two hundred years ago.

The environmentalists today are denying those technologies and those improved lives, living standards, and life spans to the poorest people on the planet. I view that as just absolutely wrong. People are as much a part of this planet as the rats and the lions and every other species. They should not be treated as second-class citizens.

The environmentalists are wrong when they say that we're no better than any of those other species: that the death of a child in Africa is no worse than the death of Cecil the Lion, and I just can't buy that. And that means anti-energy, anti-GMO, anti-bio-technology, anti-DDT, anti-pesticide policies, and anticarbon energy policies are killing literally millions of parents and children in these countries every year.

EIRNS/Stuart Lewis

The worst case of ecology/climate scares reducing population by increasing death rates. The banning of DDT 40 years ago, based on a propaganda book and a scientific study immediately invalidated by its own author, has caused 60-70 million completely preventable and deliberate deaths from malaria.

Mistaken, and Murderous, DDT Ban

Ross:: One of the things that these groups sometimes point to, they call the precautionary principle. They say that it's possible that we're going to face great threats in the future: global warming, climate change, extreme weather, the threats to bird eggshells in the case of DDT. And they say that to avoid these potential threats we have to take action now. What do you say to that?

Driessen:: Well let's start with DDT, eggshells. Professor Joel Bitman, a researcher in Maryland, did the original studies. He concluded that DDT was thinning the eggshells, and that was causing the birds to crush them and kill the embryos, and this was causing a decline in the populations of eagles and other birds. But somebody pointed out that the diet he was feeding these test birds was grossly deficient in calcium.

Well, calcium is the main component of eggshells, so Dr. Bitman, being an honest scientist, following the scientific method, went back and re-did his experiments using the proper feeds,—and there was no eggshell thinning because of DDT! But when he tried to publish those new findings, *Nature* and other science magazines refused to accept his new work for publication, because they had already taken a stand, and they were not going to back off on DDT.

So this is just one more example of the lies about DDT, but this brings you into the precautionary principle. They don't want to use DDT because some environmentalist extremists, people who are anti-pesticides, say there's a *possibility* that DDT or its metabolites like DDE might possibly have an impact on lactation in nursing mothers, or on childhood development of the brain cells, and so forth.

They don't have any evidence that this is happening, but because they raise the possibility, they say that no technology should be available, should be used, should be implemented, or brought to public access, unless they can prove that technology has none of these adverse, imaginary, imagined, exaggerated effects. They don't want to talk about the impacts of their policies or the precautionary principle itself, or the denial of these technologies.

So if you take DDT away, a million people, mothers mostly, and children, die from malaria every year. So shouldn't that be factored into the precautionary principle? There you can show a very direct link between the *lack* of this powerful insect repellent to the deaths of millions of people and the disease of malaria in billions of people over the years. And yet that's part of the precautionary principle you're not supposed to ever talk about.

It's basically a sledge-hammer that's used where the environmentalists don't like a technology, don't like living standards, don't want to let people improve their health and living standards. That's when they bring up that type of precautionary principle. They don't want it applied to their own policies, which is where it really needs to be applied.

Pope Francis' Encyclical

Ross:: Right, or a way to hide behind bad science, by saying well, it might be true. The Catholic Church is an institution that many people around the world look to as a defender of the poor and the disadvantaged. Recently, Pope Francis released the encyclical *Laudato Si'*, which takes up environmental concerns, global warming directly. What impact do you think this has? How do you see the importance of this encyclical?

Driessen:: Well it's certainly been a boost to the climate crisis crowd, the climate crisis industry. Right now they are saying that the climate crisis alarmism industry, coupled with the renewable energy industry, and others that are tied into this whole vernacular about how much carbon-based fuels are affecting earth's climate—that industry is now judged to be at about 1.5 trillion dollars a year. And you see why they want to take such a hard line on this and keep pushing this particular message.

Pope Francis, contrary to his predecessor, who didn't buy into the global warming ideas and actually rejected them, Pope Francis has accepted those pretty much hook-line-and-sinker, tied in with what he calls sustainability. He doesn't like capitalism. He doesn't like carbon-based energy. He wants to see all of that gone. He agrees with some of the leading voices in the UN, and American environmentalist movement, and the current White House under President Obama, that the United States and the whole world's economic system needs a total reformation, a total transformation. Our legal system, our constitutional system, our economic system, our energy system, should all be completely upended and replaced with who knows what. They don't really specify that.

But capitalism, free enterprise, innovation, technology, carbon-based fuels, fossil fuels, have brought the most incredible, significant transformation of the human condition in history: After thousands, tens of thousands of years of human history, over the last couple of hundred years with the industrial revolution, and coal, oil, natural gas, all of a sudden we've got living standards, and health and welfare, and lifespans better than we have ever enjoyed in history. The average person in the United States, even people on welfare, are living better than the kings and queens did a hundred, a hundred and fifty years ago.

So when Pope Francis comes in and says that we need to get rid of capitalism, we need to get rid of fossil fuels, we need to get rid of the free-enterprise system, and put a bunch of unelected, unaccountable bureaucrats in charge of everybody's living standards and lifespans, basically he means that we are going to roll back living standards in the developed world. And we're going to tell,—not *we*, but rather *they*, the ruling elites, the unelected forces that he has aligned himself with,—are going to tell the world what living standards they're going to be permitted to have.

Of course, the ruling elites will have slightly better, or a whole lot better living standards. They'll get to travel. They'll have their air-conditioning. They'll have their fancy offices, and so forth. But the average person's supposed to be held back, rolled back. The poor people of the world are going to be told, in the words of John Holdren, President Obama's Science Advisor, what level of development will be ecologically feasible as determined by these ruling elites.

And I just have a problem with that.

A Crime Against Humanity

Ross:: Returning to your examples about how power availability has transformed the lives of people. If you think about Germany, where the installed capacity of both solar and wind is over 10 gigawatts each, and the power prices are around—the last number I heard—about 37 cents a kilowatt-hour, dramatically higher than, in fact, about three or four times higher than a typical U.S. rate. You can see the cut-backs that come when you try to implement this policy. What is possible in an economy that doesn't have energy?

Driessen:: Well, you can see what's possible in an economy that doesn't have energy by going to a lot of African countries where people basically have nothing. They've still got the huts they've been living in for centuries, for millennia. They cook and heat with wood and dung and charcoal fires, animal dung. Their babies and infants are strapped on their backs breathing the same polluted smoke from those fires. They have millions of deaths every year from lung infections. Millions more deaths from unsafe drinking water and spoiled food: again, because they don't have the energy, reliable, affordable, abundant, carbon-based energy that we enjoy and benefit from.

Back to Germany for just a moment. The 37 cents per kilowatt-hour that you're talking about is the subsidized rate. Take the subsidies out and it's more like 70 or 80 cents a kilowatt-hour, compared to 8 cents a kilowatt-hour in West Virginia, which is right now 95% reliant on coal. And it's coal produced in power plants that have scrubbers; very little pollution comes out of them. What you see coming out of the stacks is water vapor and carbon dioxide, and let's always remember that water vapor comes down as rain and carbon dioxide is plant fertilizer.

Nothing on planet Earth would be here, including ourselves and the trees out here, without carbon dioxide. And the more we have in the atmosphere, the better, the faster, the more robustly, plants and crops grow.

So those are all things that need to be taken into account, when you're telling these countries in Africa, as President Obama has, that we're not going to provide

And people are going to be kept in those impoverished conditions for the foreseeable future, under those policies. I find that inhumane, a crime against humanity, and just immoral. We can't allow it.

loans or grants to build fossil fuel power plants, and they need to get by on wind and solar, which are far pricier. It's energy when it's available, rather than when you need it. It's basically telling them: put a solar panel on your hut, and have a one cubic foot refrigerator, and a light bulb, and a charging station for your cell phone, and that's the most that we're going to allow you to develop. Or have a wind turbine for your village: again, energy when it's available not when it's needed. And people are going to be kept in those impoverished conditions for the foreseeable future, under those policies. I find that inhumane, a crime against humanity, and just immoral. We can't allow it.

The Paris Conference

Ross:: Right. On the political front, there is another Conference of Parties conference coming up in Paris at the end of this year. And there is a major push to get an agreement on reducing CO2 emissions at this conference. Do you have any thoughts on this upcoming conference?

Driessen:: Well, first of all, whatever is going to come out of it from our perspective here in the United States is going to be a treaty. Not an agreement, not some little scrap of paper. It's going to be a binding commitment, a binding treaty between the United States and other countries, and with the United Nations, if President Obama gets his way, and gets something like that developed and agreed to by all these various nations.

That means it needs a two-thirds vote by the Senate; it's not a two-thirds vote of disapproval, but a two-thirds vote of approval. I don't think that's ever going to happen, and I think we need to let the world know that the United States is not going to become a party to some treaty that binds us and tells us we need to roll back our energy use, our carbon dioxide emissions, and our living standards to satisfy the climate cartel, the climate crisis industry.

I think also you're looking at a lot of countries that are only going to sign this because they think they're going to share in this hundred *billion* dollar a year transfer of wealth from developed countries, or what I call FRCs (Formerly Rich Countries) because we've already battered our economies so much with these anti-technology, anti-energy policies. I don't think that money's going to be there, number one, but this is what these countries expect, and that's the number one reason they're looking to sign an agreement like this. They want what they call climate mitigation adaptation and reparation money.

So, even if the money does come, or even if a portion of that comes, the other thing that the people in these developing countries need to know, the ones that are being held back right now, by all these policies against them building fossil fuel power plants, is that it's not going to be the average person in these countries that gets any of that money.

That money is going to end up in the pockets and the Swiss bank accounts of the ruling elites. And the average person is going to get nothing. Maybe, as I said, a solar panel on a hut. And they're going to continue to live pretty miserably and die young, be exposed to the same diseases they are fighting day after day right now. So I don't think this is going to be a good deal.

Moreover, the way it's structured, it's only going to be countries like the United States that will be bound, required to roll back their energy use, or carbon dioxide emissions in their living standards. So countries like China and India and Indonesia, every other country, are going to be building coal-fired power plants at the rate of a power plant a week, or faster, and the carbon dioxide levels in the earth's atmosphere will continue to rise. So even if you believe that carbon dioxide has replaced all the incredibly complex, interrelated, powerful natural forces that have ruled climate change from Earth's beginnings throughout human history—even if you believe that,—the carbon dioxide level in the Earth's atmosphere is going to continue to increase, and whatever the United States does will have no impact whatsoever on Earth's climate.

And in fact, even EPA has admitted that the policies it's jamming down our throats right now, that are killing jobs all over the United States, impoverishing families, raising energy priceseven with all those policies, EPA says that 85 years from now, the year 2100, they will have prevented global warming to the tune of 0.03 degrees Fahrenheit, not even one-tenth of one degree; you can't even measure this stuff!

So this is what we're looking at coming out of the Obama Administration in the form of EPA regulations and/or a climate treaty. That's a bad deal for us. We think the Iran deal is bad. This is just as bad or worse, and it will have repercussions throughout our economy. Poor and minority families are going to get hit the hardest. Blue collar families will see their jobs, their industries wiped out. And again it will only be the ruling classes that benefit from this.

Not a good idea.

Abri le Roux

A rooftop solar water heater in South Africa. Supporting installation of such devices, rather than large-scale energy resources, as a policy of "appropriate technology" is inhuman.

Turning Back the Clock

Ross:: I'd like to return to your theme about the disgusting immorality of these actions, of telling countries, No, you can't develop. You're not able to live as a full person. One field of human thought where there are expressed concepts about man's role in nature, the concept of human identity, is in religion. And Martin Palmer, an aide of Prince Philip's, had worked with him in 1986, to set up an alliance of conservation and religion, to get religions to accept the idea that human beings were not the center of the world, not that important, just another living species. And he had said that this would have difficulty among Judaism, Christianity, and Islam.

He particularly singled out Christianity for mingling of the divine and the human, and the idea of human beings as a creative force. It's not accidental in view of these actions, that religion and global warming seem connected in the fact that the global warming alarmists seem to have an almost religious conviction about the proper number of human beings on the planet, the identity of the human race, and what we deserve to have. Any thoughts on this?

Driessen:: Yeah, absolutely. Essentially what Palmer and too many others,—and even Pope Francis is getting pulled into this maelstrom—they're trying to replace Judeo-Christianity and other religions with a return to nature worship of Gaia as the earth mother, of nature as a god unto itself. And they reject the real teachings of Christianity and Judaism, and so forth, that man is here obligated to be a responsible steward of Earth and God's creation, and to use Earth's and God's bounteous resources to improve the lot of human beings, to improve the environment.

If you go back a couple of centuries, or you look around the cities in Third World countries, you don't find much in the way of forests. You find degradation, you find pollution, you find waterways and air really polluted by massive amounts of disease; you find people still dying at age 35 or 45 on average, rather than 75 or 85. It's because they don't have the kinds of technologies we have developed and made our everyday existence in the United States and Europe.

Just imagine, try to imagine your life without electricity 24/7/365: affordable, abundant for whatever you need it for. Just running your cell phone, your modern day cell phone, your laptop, and so forth. The amount of energy required, not just to charge it,—that's piddling,—but to operate the infrastructure, the servers; the whole base of knowledge that you're feeding into that telephone everyday is enormous. You cannot do that with wind and solar power.

Even Google's top scientists, after spending a couple of years looking into this, finally admitted that fossil fuels were required and that wind and solar were not going to be able to cut it, that not even the Google technology was going to make it with just wind and solar.[1] Think about your hospitals, your factories, your small businesses, your malls, your schools, your own house, operating only with wind and solar power.

And keep in mind that the same people that hate fossil fuels, who hate any carbon-based energy, and are crazy about global warming, they also detest nuclear power, hydroelectric, anything that really can provide more reliable affordable energy, they're against it. They want the energy for themselves, again, but they don't want other people to have it.

What Scarce Resources?

Ross:: Are we running out of resources? Is there anything to that concern?

Driessen:: You look around and we've got a very big planet. We haven't run out of anything yet. Paul Ehrlich had that famous bet with Julian Simon that the price of resources, that Ehrlich himself chose, would actually go down over the couple of years succeeding the bet, and Ehrlich lost the bet to Simon. Simon said the price was going to go down. Ehrlich said it would go up. And it went down for every one of those, because we found more efficient ways to find and extract those resources.

Fracking, the hydraulic fracturing revolution. Whoever would have dreamed that the United States would be the number one gas-producing, and almost number one oil-producing nation in the world after all the craziness of the '70s with the OPEC oil embargo and President Carter saying, We all just have to cut out our use of fossil fuels. We're running out and we face an environmental and resource crisis. Well, we've got an awful lot of those resources, instead of the stories of peak oil and of us running out in a couple of years. (And by the way, the U.S. geological survey first said that we were going to run out oil back in 1923. So this has been around for a long time.)

And the notion that we have hit peak oil has been completely obliterated by the fracking revolution. That's the real reason the environmentalists don't like fracking. Peak oil, like the climate crisis and the pollution and precaution—those are the pillars of the environmentalist movement. And we've just knocked one of them out from under them, showing that *the resources are really first there in the minds of human beings*. You first find oil in the *mind* of the explorer.

Creative Commons

A solar water pump in Morocco. Can an advanced industrial nation be built by assembling such low-energy parts?

Julian Simon always called the creative innovative human mind the ultimate resource. To master resources, energy, affordable, reliable, abundant energy, *the ultimate resource is our creative minds*, and our ability to find new ways to do things, new resources. We didn't end the stone age because we ran out of stones. And we didn't end the bronze age because we ran out of bronze.

What we're going to run out of is the resources that the environmentalists, the Obama Administration, and other people in government, prevent us from getting access to. If they close off the land, and say you can't go in there and explore; if they close off the ocean areas, and you can't go in there and explore and drill; if you can't find the rare earths that I am absolutely positive we have in great abundance right here in the United States, but nobody's allowed to go into the places where they are likely to be foundif these are prohibited, then you are going to run out.

And the prices are going to go up and people are going to do without. Their living standards, their jobs, everything's going to be decimated. People are going to die earlier. *And it's not because we are running out resources, it's because certain groups prevent us from finding and developing the resources that we need for a modern science and technology.*

Going back to this whole notion of sustainability: Gro Brundtland, who was Premier of Norway, and became very high in the United Nations, had a definition of sustainability: that current generations should only use the resources that are not going to affect the needs of future generations. Well, how do you do that?

1. The report by the Google researchers is linked here.

I grew up a few miles from the first house in the world to be powered by hydroelectric electricity. I look around at all these technologies, just in my life or the life of my father (who was almost 97 a year ago when he died): airplanes, cell-phones, computers, laptops, the amazing computing power you have in that little bitty cell-phone that you are taking around now, video cameras, everything we make and do and use today, is a brand new technology that basically didn't exist a few years ago. How do you predict today what technologies future generations are going to have and therefore what raw materials they are going to need to make those technologies? It cannot be done.

So the whole concept of sustainability as a political force, as a political ideology, is stupid and unworkable, and is being used as another hammer to keep people pounded down and prevent them from improving their living standards and well-being.

Stand Up and Be Counted

Ross:: With all the problems in sustainability, environmentalism, and the failure of these power schemes, why is it that this ideology has taken hold? What's missing in people's understanding that made this possible?

Driessen:: Well I think what's missing is what the hard-core environmentalists don't want to talk about, which is the human, the real human and real environmental impacts of their policies, of their ideologies, of the regulations that they're imposing on us....

So to me, our job is to stand up and not be silenced. Bring up these inconvenient truths, these inconvenient questions, force them to deal with it. Al Gore will not debate anybody on climate change. He won't even take a question that he has not pre-approved before his little lectures on climate. Hillary Clinton refuses to be interviewed on anything. Barack Obama gets very petulant and petty when somebody asks him a tough question. And you see this all the way across the environmental movement, the UN, Michael Mann, any of these people that are involved in sustainability, climate alarmism, and so forth, the transformation of the world's economic system, like Cristiana Figueres, the head of the UN's Climate Organization—they don't want to talk about any of these inconvenient, troublesome crimes against humanity that I bring up.

And we need to do this over and over. And we need to tell the stories of the people whose lives are being destroyed, whose children are dying, who themselves are dying, because of these anti-energy, anti-insecticide, anti-fertilizer, anti-GMO policies that are being jammed down their throats by these baby-killers. These are good technologies. Obviously sometimes you can have a technology that's abused, or accidents happen. But to say that these technologies should just be eliminated because of that and replaced with who-knows-what or replaced with nothing?...

I think it needs a real serious house-cleaning in the UN, the EPA. Let people know what the environmental movement has become.

So I think there's a lot of work to be done. But I'm glad you're doing this and glad we all have an opportunity to stand up and be counted.

Ross:: Paul Driessen, thanks a lot.

Driessen:: Thank you, Jason.

Temperature Doesn't Follow CO_2 As Alarmists Claim

by Benjamin Deniston

Aug. 3, 2015—Those supporting the narrative of an impending man-made climate change catastrophe base this on an assertion that the Earth's climate is extremely sensitive to increases in CO_2 emissions and that CO_2 ranks high among the most important factors determining climate across many timescales. When you hear about rising human CO_2 emissions causing everything from devastating droughts to worsening storms, from sea level rise to mass extinctions, realize that these are all based on computer models built on the assertion that changes in CO_2 will have a strong effect on global climate. However, there is one minor problem with their arguments: reality does not support that assertion.

FIGURE 1

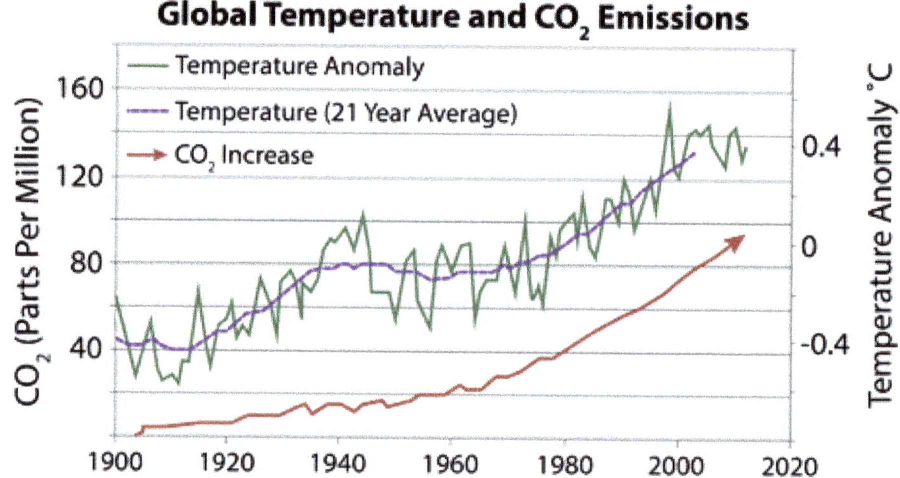

The annual average global temperature is from the Hadley Center in the United Kingdom. The cumulative emissions are from the international inventory data base of the USA Department of Energy. The CO_2 levels prior to 1959 are from NOAA records of Antarctic ice cores, and CCO_2 levels after 1959 are from measurements at Mauna Loa, Hawaii. CO_2 increases are measured above a 1900 baseline value of 300 parts per million (by volume). Graphic adapted from an original by Ferdinand Engelbeen.

The climate is always changing, with many factors involved (as discussed in the accompanying article, "What Causes Climate Change? The Sun, the Solar System, and the Galaxy"), and the historical and geological evidence tells us that CO_2 is a relatively *minor* factor (if much of a factor at all).

Case 1: 20th Century

Start by comparing CO_2 levels and temperature over the past century. From 1900 to the present the relation between the claimed human greenhouse gas emissions and the yearly average global temperature is far from self-evident. **Figure 1** compares global average temperature with increases in greenhouse gas and CO_2 emissions (above a baseline of 300 parts per million).

The data shows global temperature increase from 1910 to 1945, during a period when human greenhouse emissions were relatively low. As the rate of CO_2 increase began to accelerate over the following 30 years, global temperatures did not increase along with them; the temperatures went flat from 1945 to 1975. The only period where these processes correspond is the recent warming phase, from 1975 to 1998. However, since 1998 global temperatures have again gone flat, breaking from the upward trend in CO_2 emissions.

Before going on, it should be emphasized that this disagreement is evident in the most recent historical data provided by NOAA and other government agencies. As will be discussed in the accompanying article, "The 'Methods' of Climate Alarmists," we have strong reasons to question the accuracy of the historical data provided by government agencies with a vested interest in the man-made climate change catastrophe narrative, as they have been seen to repeatedly cherry-pick the data that supports their assertions, or even "adjust" historical data to fit their claims. That stated, even with these biases in the data selection and adjustment processes, we *still* see this disagreement between CO_2 and temperature.

FIGURE 2

Satellite Data Shows No Global Temperature Rise for 18 Years

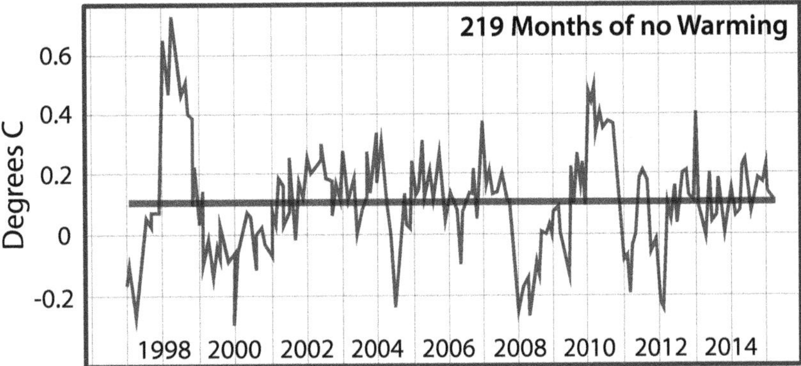

Global Lower Troposphere Temperature Anomalies from UAH (University of Alabama in Huntsville) Analysis of Satellite Data
(Version 6.0 beta; January 1997 to March 2015; Reference 1981-2010)

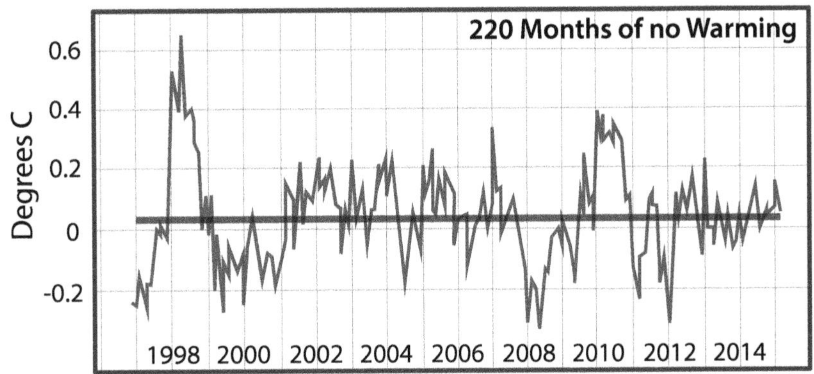

Global Lower Troposphere Temperature Anomalies from RSS (Remote Sensing Systems) Analysis of Satellite Data
(December 1996 to March 2015; Reference 1979-1998)

The RSS (Remote Sensing Systems) and UAH (University of Alabama in Huntsville) analysis of satellite measurements show that there has been no trend of global temperature increase since the late 1990s. Graphics reproduced from originals by Bob Tisdale.

Case 2: The Pause

Focusing on this more recent period (1998 to the present), two different assessments of global temperature based on satellite measurements both show that global temperatures have shown no increasing trend since 1998 – despite the relatively large increase in CO_2 levels. These satellite measurements represent an important, independent temperature record, free from the manipulations discussed in the accompanying article, "The 'Methods' of Climate Alarmists."

This recent flat-line in global temperature has been popularized as the global warming "pause" or "hiatus." Even with CO_2 and other greenhouse emissions continuing to accelerate over the past two decades, *the Earth hasn't warmed in response*. While there are literally dozens of purported explanations for why this pause shouldn't question the narrative that the climate is extremely sensitive to CO_2 levels and continued human CO_2 emissions will cause catastrophic climate change, the simple fact of the matter is that these are all post hoc excuses. *None of the climate models predicted this pause before it occurred, and now you're being told to trust those same climate models for future predictions of how CO_2 increases will devastate the Earth's climate.*

The spectacular failure of computer models to ac-

FIGURE 3

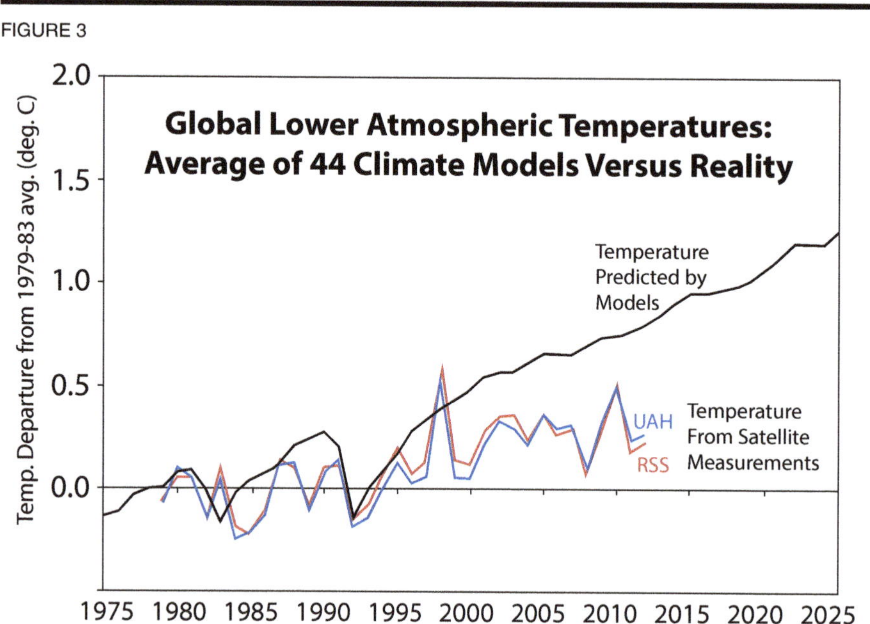

"The global temperature predicted by an average of 44 climate models compared against actual global temperatures measured by satellites. Image adapted from Dr. Roy Spencer, "95% of Climate Models Agree: The Observations Must be Wrong," February 7th, 2014, http://www.drroyspencer.com/

FIGURE 4

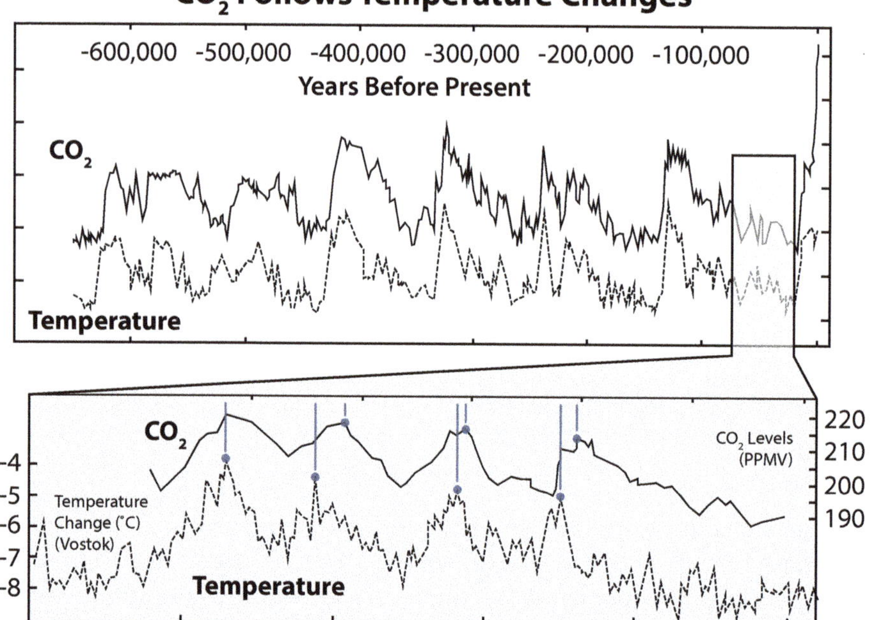

Measurements of temperature and CO_2 for the past 600,000 years. When the entire period is viewed, a very clear correlation is apparent, but which is causing the other to change? When examined more closely, we see that temperature changes first, followed by changes in CO_2 levels (which appear to be responding to the temperature changes). Image adapted from "Analysis of ice core data from Antarctica," by Indermühle et al. (GRL, vol. 27, p. 735, 2000), and the science fiction film An Inconvenient Truth.

curately predict how the Earth's climate will respond to changes in CO_2 levels can be further illustrated by comparing the predictions made by dozens of computer models with the actual results that occurred. As can be seen in **Figure 3**, actual temperature has remained below the vast majority of all climate model predictions, and well below the average of all predictions.

These results indicate that the Earth's climate is not responding to CO_2 emissions as claimed by those supporting the man-made climate change crisis narrative. Surprised? You shouldn't be. This is completely consistent with the picture we get from historical and geological records – a climate that is not highly responsive to CO_2 levels. On certain timescales we see the *opposite* of what we're generally told by alarmists, CO_2 levels being determined by climate (rather than CO_2 determining climate).

Case 3: CO_2 Lags Behind Temperature

One of the more infamous illustrations of this comes from the evidence popularized by none other than Al Gore in his science fiction film, *An Inconvenient Truth*. Gore presented a close correlation between CO_2 levels and temperature records going back a half million years (recorded in ice core samples from Antarctica). This was presented as conclusive evidence that CO_2 changes drive changes in global temperature, with Gore stating "there is one relationship that is far more powerful than all the others, and it is this: when there is more carbon dioxide the temperature gets warmer, because it traps more heat from the Sun inside."

However, what Gore didn't mention was that it was already known that the changes in CO_2 levels came *after* changes in temperature, indicating that CO_2 was not causing the climate to change, but only *responding* to temperature change. This is no surprise. The oceans absorb, store, and release large amounts of CO_2, and because the ocean temperature determines how much CO2 can be stored, changes in climate (and ocean temperature) can increase or decrease the CO_2 in the atmosphere. For example, warming causes more CO_2 to be released into the atmosphere, so a CO_2 increase would be expected to come after (lag behind) a temperature rise.[1]

Records of CO_2 changes following temperatures have repeatedly been shown in multiple studies. A 1999 study showed that CO_2 changes followed behind temperature changes by 600 years during the last three transitions from ice ages to interglacial periods.[2] A 2000 study found that CO_2 lagged temperature changes by 1,200 years in Antarctic ice cores between 60,000 and 20,000 years ago (see **Figure 4**).[3] A 2001 study demonstrated an 800 year CO_2 lag in the beginning of the most recent interglacial. And a 2005 study showed CO_2 lagging temperature changes in temperature by 1,900 years in Antarctic data.

FIGURE 5

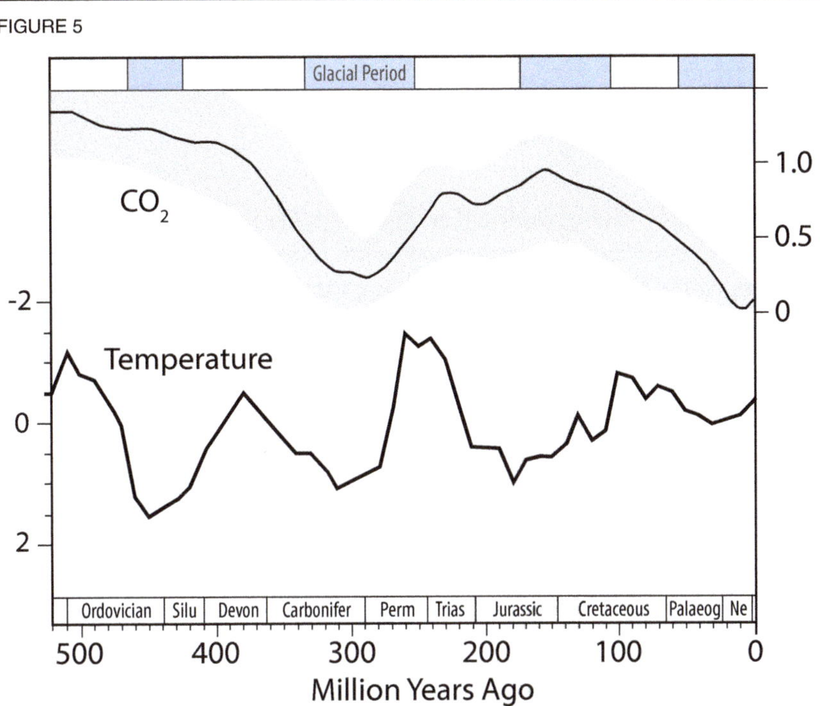

Temperature and CO_2 levels for the past 500 million years. Image adapted from Berner and Kothavala, 2001 and Veizer et al., 2001.

Case 4: The Phanerozoic

The lack of climate sensitivity to CO_2 is further supported when we look at longer timescales, covering hundreds of millions of years. For records covering the entire time of advanced animal life on Earth (the Phanerozoic Eon, from 540 million years ago to the present) we see no evidence that CO_2 changes drive global climate. We see periods where CO_2 levels were much higher than today, with lower global temperatures (as in the Ordovician and Jurassic periods). And we see long term trends of CO_2 increase associated with temperature decrease, following by CO_2 decrease being associated with temperature increase (from the late Permian, through the Triassic, Jurassic, and Cretaceous). Again, this shows the absurdity of the assertion that the Earth's climate is highly responsive to atmospheric CO_2 levels, and the criminality of the alarmists demands that human CO_2 emissions be drastically cut back.

Whether we look at the recent changes of the Earth's climate over the past decades and centuries, or longer term records covering the past hundreds of thousands or hundreds of millions of years, we see clear evidence demonstrating that CO_2 is not a major factor determining the Earth's climate. As discussed in the accompanying article, "What Causes Climate Change? The Sun, the Solar System, and the Galaxy."

Bottom line: is CO_2 a greenhouse gas? Yes. Could an increase in CO_2 levels affect the climate? Sure, that is possible, but the evidence indicates it wouldn't be much of an effect (if any). Is there any reason to believe that human CO_2 emissions are going to bring the world climate system to the verge of some catastrophic change? *Absolutely not.*

1. Many supporters of the man-made climate change crisis narrative don't dispute that CO_2 changes follow behind temperature changes, but they argue that different causes (other than CO_2) initiate the temperature change, which then releases more CO_2, and then CO_2 acts to amplify these temperature changes. However, this is just reasserting their thesis, and providing no proof. According to this scenario these geological records don't provide any evidence to support the claim that the climate is highly sensitive to CO_2 change (as Gore claimed).
2. Fischer et al., *Science*, vol 283, p. 1712, 1999.
3. Indermühle et al., GRL, vol. 27, p. 735, 2000.

What Causes Climate Change? The Sun, the Solar System, and the Galaxy

by Benjamin Deniston

Aug. 3, 2015—Where historical and geological records of CO_2 changes fail to correspond with temperature changes, shifts in the activity of the Sun, the characteristics of the Solar System, and the Sun's position within the Galaxy do match climate and related changes quite well. This can be clearly seen on a series of different timescales.

On the timescale of the past century, variations in Solar activity match changes in the Earth's temperature (which clearly deviate from the trends in CO_2 emissions). This has been shown with measurements of average US temperature, average Arctic temperature, and average global temperature, compared with changes in solar activity. From around 1900 the temperature increased until about the middle of the century – when CO_2 emissions were relatively low, *but solar activity was on the rise*. From about the 1940s to the mid-1970s, temperature held flat, or even declined – matching the easing of solar activity, but not matching the accelerated increase in CO_2 emissions. The warming from the mid-1970s to the end of the century matches both the increase in solar activity and the increase in CO_2 emissions, but since the turn of the century solar activity has leveled off and temperature has leveled off with it (while CO_2 emissions continue to accelerate)(**Figure 1**).

While it has been argued that the measured changes in the amount of sunlight reaching the Earth are too small to account for the observed global climate change, a new body of research is showing that there is an additional process which amplifies the effect of the Sun on the Earth's climate: the Sun's role in affecting the flux of galactic cosmic radiation, which plays a critical role in cloud formation (and, therefore, cli-

FIGURE 1

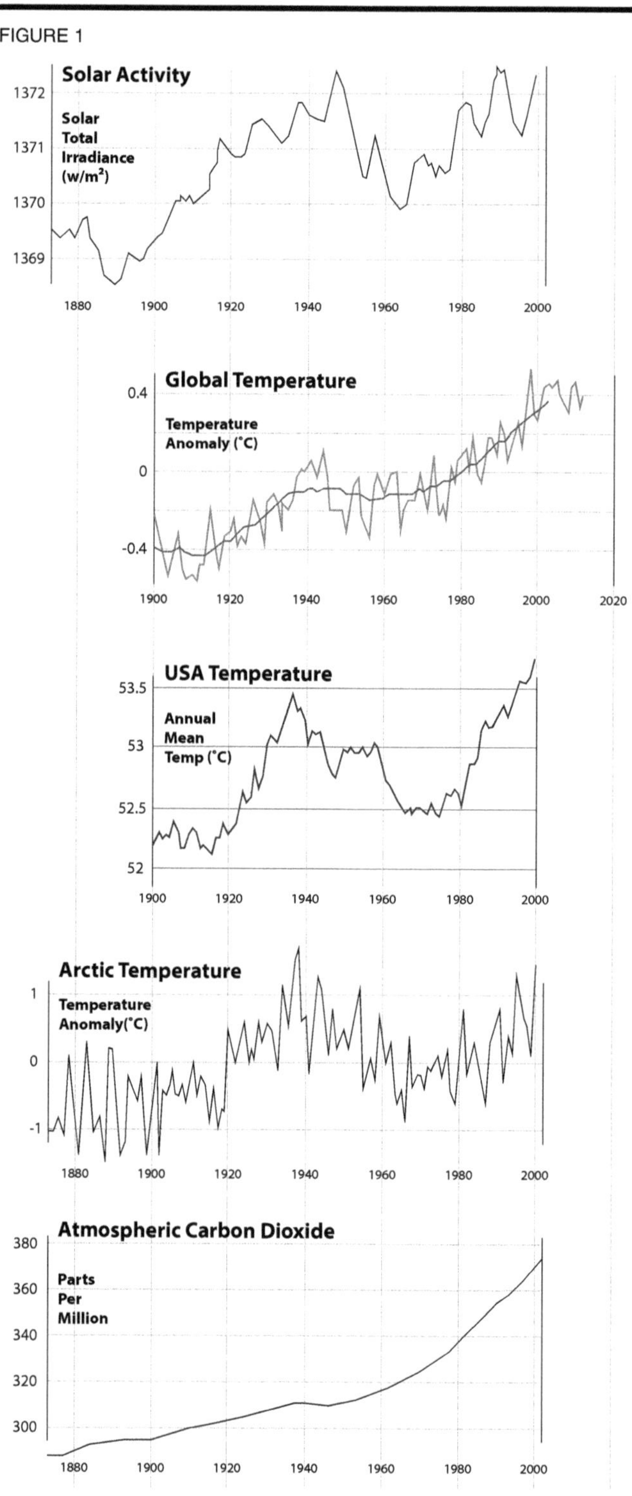

Three different temperature records over the past century show the same general trends: warming in the first half of the century, leveling off or cooling from the 1940s to 1970s, followed by warming which lasted until about the turn of the century. This matches the general changes in solar activity, as measured by the sunlight reaching the Earth (total solar irradiance), but not changes in CO_2 emissions.

FIGURE 2A

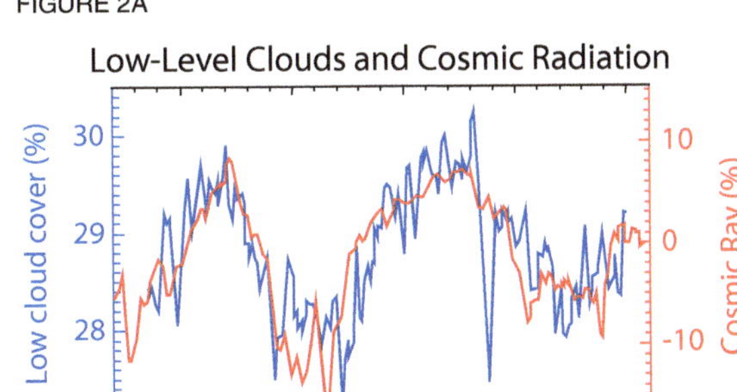

FIGURE 2B

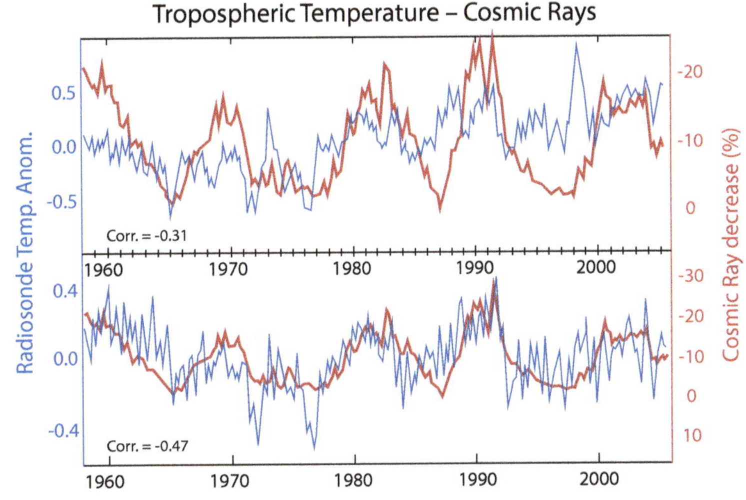

FIGURE 2C

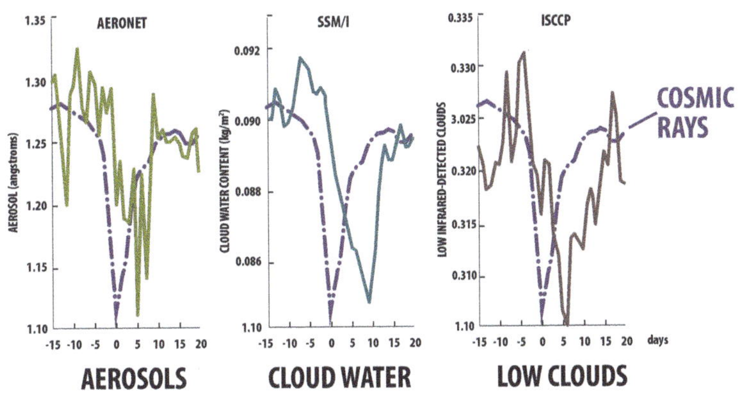

Svensmark, H. and Friis-Christensen, E., "Reply to Lockwood and Fröhlich – The persistent role of the Sun in climate forcing", Danish National Space Center Scientific Report 3/2007.

Various atmospheric processes have been shown to respond to changes in the flux of galactic cosmic radiation. This includes low-level cloud formation and atmospheric temperature, as measured over past decades, as well as aerosol formation and the water content in clouds, as measured days after sharp drops in the flux of galactic cosmic radiation. Graphic adapted from originals in Svensmark, H. and Friis-Christensen, E., "Reply to Lockwood and Fröhlich – The persistent role of the Sun in climate forcing", Danish National Space Center Scientific Report 3/2007; and "Cosmic ray decreases affect atmospheric aerosols and clouds," Henrik Svensmark, Torsten Bondo, Jacob Svensmark, Geophysical Research Letters, 2009, 36 (15).

mate). Galactic cosmic radiation is composed of atomic particles (mostly protons and helium nuclei, with a few nuclei of heavier elements as well) traveling at extremely high speeds throughout the galaxy. Because they are charged, the Sun's magnetic field acts to change their paths, thereby regulating the amount of high energy galactic cosmic radiation reaching the Earth's atmosphere – a stronger Sun means the Earth receives less galactic cosmic radiation, and a weaker Sun means the Earth receives more.

In 1997 Danish scientists Henrik Svensmark and Eigil Friis-Christensen showed that the density of low-level cloud cover appeared to change in response to variations in the flux of galactic cosmic radiation. Since then they continued to develop evidence to support their new theory, showing in laboratory experiments that galactic cosmic radiation affects the processes which lead to cloud formation,[1] and identifying additional responses of the Earth's climate system to changes in the cosmic radiation flux. In a 2007 study Svensmark and Friis-Christensen showed that the global average temperature of the atmosphere rose and fell in lock step with changes in the flux of galactic cosmic radiation. In a 2009 study Svensmark and colleagues showed that the number of low level clouds, the water content in clouds, and the number of cloud forming aerosols all decreased in the days following sudden drops in galactic cosmic radiation (caused by explosive outbursts of solar magnetic activity) (**Figure 2**).

These studies all show that cosmic radiation plays a critical role in processes of cloud formation and thereby

1. "Response of cloud condensation nuclei (>50 nm) to changes in ion-nucleation," Henrik Svensmark, Martin B. Enghoff, Jens Olaf Pepke Pedersen, *Physics Letters A*, Volume 377, Issue 37, 8 November 2013, Pages 2343–2347.

FIGURE 3

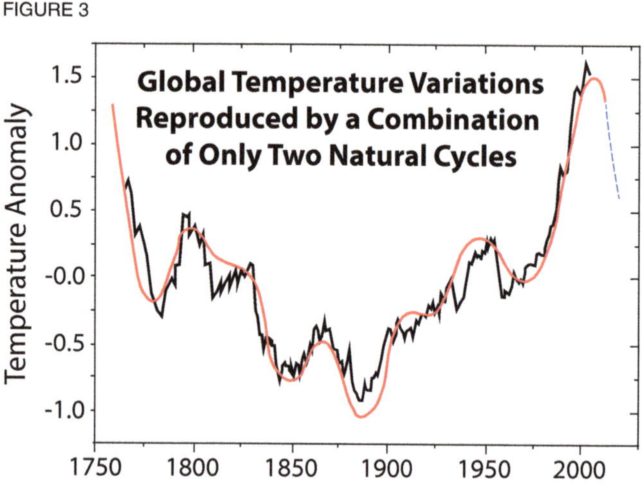

"Cosmic ray decreases affect atmospheric aerosols and clouds," Henrik Svensmark, Torsten Bondo, Jacob Svensmark, Geophysical Research Letters, 2009; 36 (15).

The interaction of only two cycles, those of 210 and 65 years, produces the red curve, matching recorded temperature changes extremely well. Graphic adapted from original by Lüdecke et al.

FIGURE 4

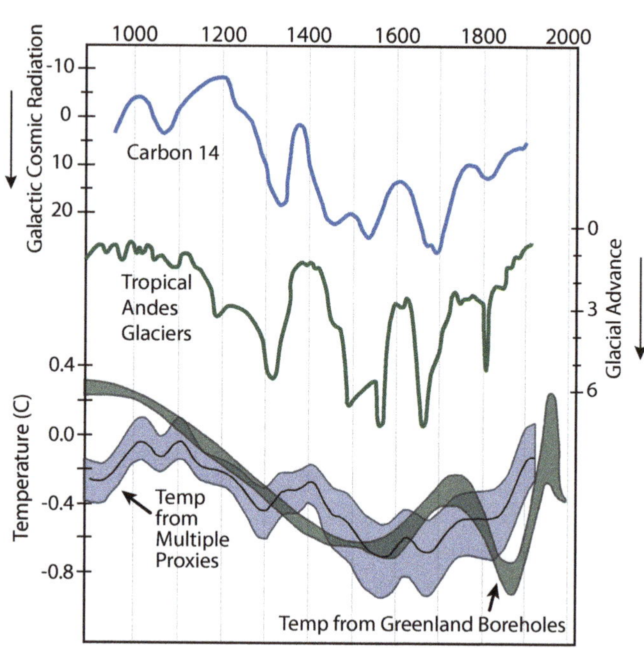

Image adapted from "Cosmic Rays and Climate," by Jasper Kirkby, Surveys in Geophysics 28, *333–375.*

acts as a critical factor in determining the Earth's climate, because clouds regulate the amount of sunlight reaching the Earth's surface. A more active Sun not only puts out more light, but it also blocks more cosmic radiation, meaning fewer clouds and more sunlight reaching the Earth's surface. Svensmark and colleagues have shown that just a few percent change in low level cloud cover (attributable to change in the flux of galactic cosmic radiation) could account for half of the warming in the past century.

This relatively new body of work indicates that much of the climate change over the past century has been largely driven by natural activity, meaning any effect human CO_2 emissions have had is relatively negligible, and future human CO_2 emissions are not something to worry about. This conclusion is supported by a recent study from a group in Germany which looked for cycles in temperature records covering the last few hundred years. In their own analysis they clearly identified the presence of two already known cycles, an approximately 200 year cycle in solar activity (known as the "Suess cycle" or "de Vries cycle") and an approximately 65 year cycle in Atlantic ocean temperatures (known as the "Atlantic Multidecadal Oscillation"). When they examined the interaction of these two natural cycles they found that just these two cycles alone accounted for most of the climate change over the past centuries, including the recent warming trends – again, indicating that there is little evidence CO_2 has an effect worth worrying about.[2] (**Figure 3**).

With this in mind, let's look a bit further back in time. If we examine records of climate over the past few thousand years we again see that climate changes match records of variations in galactic cosmic ray flux (and not changes in CO_2). Multiple records of climate over the past thousand years indicate lower temperatures from the 1500s to the 1800s, corresponding to a period of lower solar activity and increased galactic cosmic rays. Additionally, during this time we see periods of increased glaciation in the Andes Mountains, matching periodic increases in galactic cosmic ray flux quite well. Prior to this, from around the 900s to the 1200s the temperature was warmer (the Medieval Warm Period), galactic cosmic ray flux was less, and glaciation in the Andes was less (see **Figure 4**).

2 "Multi-periodic climate dynamics: spectral analysis of long-term instrumental and proxy temperature records," H.-J. Lüdecke, A. Hempelmann, and C. O. Weiss, *Climate of the Past*, February 22, 2013. "Paleoclimate forcing by the solar De Vries/Suess cycle," H.-J. Lüdeckel, C. O. Weiss, and A. Hempelmann, *Climate of the Past*, February 12, 2015.

Looking at the past two thousand years, temperature records from the Alps follow changes in galactic cosmic rays very well – while, again, changes in CO_2 levels don't match the temperature records, changing in the opposite directions for hundreds of years (see **Figure 5**).[3]

These records from the past one and two thousand years confirm the picture developed from examining the past 100 years, that changes in the flux of galactic cosmic radiation (regulated by solar activity) govern changes in the climate, not CO_2.

Stepping back even further in time, we see more evidence of galactic cosmic radiation being a driving factor in climate change. An examination of the galactic cosmic radiation flux over the entirety of the current interglacial period (the Holocene epoch, lasting from 12,000 years ago to the present) shows a very strong relation to records of variations in glaciation and ice flow in the Northern Atlantic Ocean.[4] Additionally, shifting to a slightly finer resolution, records of variations in long-term trends in precipitation in the Arabian Peninsula, measured from 6,200 years ago to 9,600 years ago, show a *very strong* relationship to variations in galactic cosmic radiation flux.[5] **Figure 6**

Taken together, we have evidence that critical factors in the Earth's climate system respond to changes in galactic cosmic radiation on timescales of days, years, decades, centuries, and millennia – demonstrated in independent studies.

Shifting to longer timescales, the cycles of transition between ice ages and shorter interglacial periods are closely associated with changes in the *Earth's orbit* around the Sun and with changes in the *tilt* and *orientation* of the Earth's spin axis – together known as the Milankovitch Cycles. For the past one

FIGURE 5

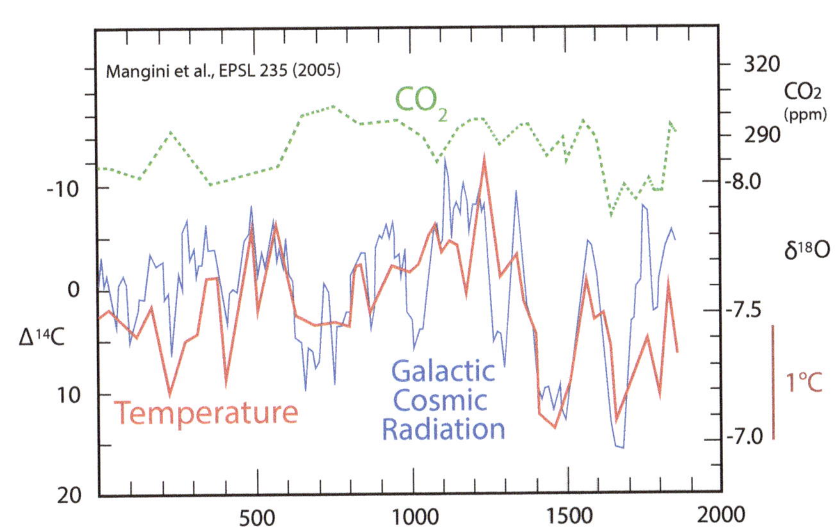

Image adapted from "Cosmic Rays and Climate," by Jasper Kirkby, Surveys in Geophysics 28, *333–375.*

FIGURE 6

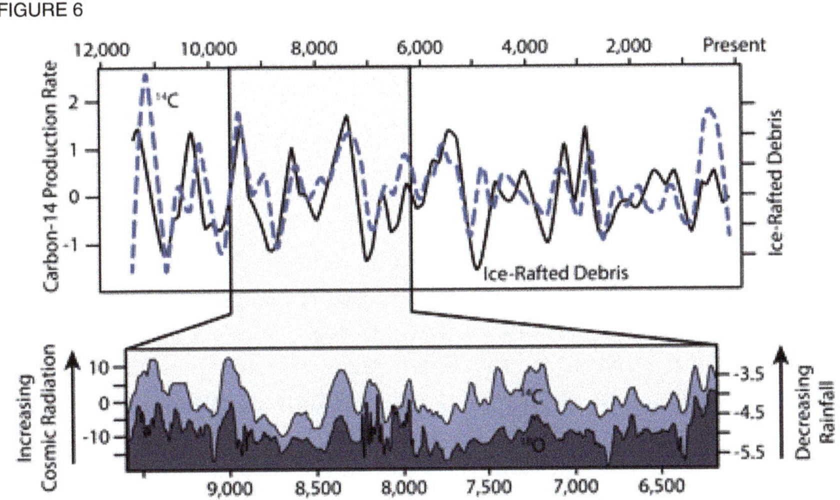

Variations in the flux of cosmic radiation over the past 12,000 years are measured by changes in the amount of carbon-14 produced. These cosmic radiation fluctuations match variations in glaciation and ice flow in the northern Atlantic Ocean (measured by ice-rafted debris) and variations in rainfall in the Arabian Peninsula. Graphics adapted from Bond et al., "Persistent solar influence on North Atlantic climate during the Holocene," Science 294, 2130–2136 (2001); and Neff et al., "Strong coincidence between solar variability and the monsoon in Oman between 9 and 6 ky ago," Nature 411, 290–293 (2001).

3. "Cosmic Rays and Climate," Jasper Kirkby, *Surveys in Geophysics*, February 28, 2008
4. Bond, et al., "Persistent solar influence on North Atlantic climate during the Holocene," *Science* **294**, 2130-2136 (2001); Kirkby, *op cit.*
5. Neff,et al., "Strong coincidence between solar variability and the monsoon in Oman between 9 and 6 ky ago," *Nature* **411**, 290-293 (2001).

FIGURE 7

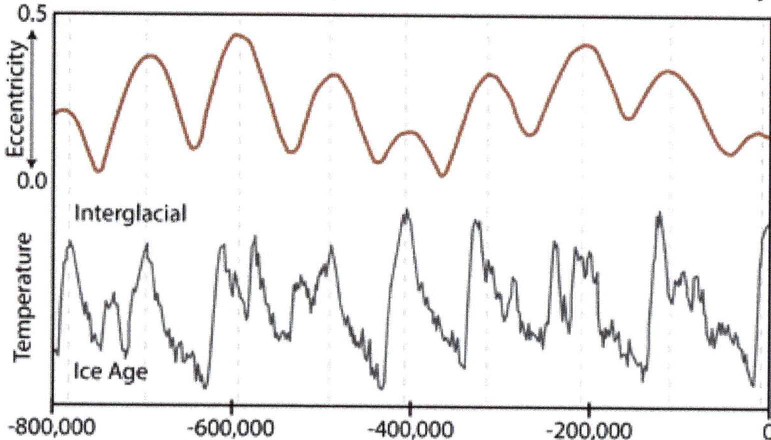

Over the past one million years, changes in the eccentricity of the Earth's orbit around the Sun match the periodic climate changes from ice ages to relatively brief interglacial periods.

million years ice age cycles have had the strongest correlation with changes in the eccentricity of the Earth's orbit around the Sun. For the two million years prior (from three to one million years ago) the Earth's climate changes best correlated with changes in the tilt of the Earth's axis. **Figure 7**

Taking one more step to larger timescales, even larger climate changes over tens and hundreds of millions of years correspond with the motion of our Solar System through the galaxy – likely due to larger changes in galactic cosmic radiation flux. While changes in the strength of the Sun's magnetic field modulate the amount of galactic cosmic radiation on the order of ten percent, in different regions of the galaxy the Solar System (and the Earth therein) can experience much larger fluctuations in galactic cosmic radiation – bringing changes on the order of one hundred percent. In accordance with the work of Svensmark and his associates, this larger variation in cosmic radiation flux over geological timescales should drive large-scale climate variations. This is exactly is what the records show.

Over the past 540 million years (the Phanerozoic eon) the Earth's climate has shifted back and forth four times between two general climate modes, icehouse and hothouse. During the hothouse modes there are no continental glaciers on Earth and temperatures are significantly higher. During the icehouse modes the climate is colder and glaciers develop and expand.

We are currently in an icehouse mode, with the ice sheet over Antarctica starting to form around 34 million years ago, and the Arctic ice sheets forming only two million years ago.

In 2000 scientist Ján Veizer and his associates showed that the four hothouse-icehouse transitions over the past half billion years do *not* correspond with changes in CO_2 levels, and in 2003 Veizer together with Nir Shaviv showed that these climate transitions *do* correspond with the periods of the Solar System's passage through our Galaxy's spiral arms. This is consistent with Svensmark's work, since the Galaxy's spiral arms are expected to have significantly higher concentrations of galactic cosmic radiation, and we see that the Earth's four most recent icehouse modes correspond with the times when the Solar System is thought to have been traveling through a spiral arm. Shaviv was also able to provide additional evidence by examining iron meteorites, which showed records of having been exposed to higher galactic cosmic radiation levels at times when the Solar System is believed to have been traveling through the spiral arms (recorded when the meteorites were still orbiting though interplanetary space as part of an asteroid).[6]

Together, records of higher galactic cosmic radiation flux recorded in iron meteorites, correspond with the time when we think the Solar System has been passing through the Galaxy's spiral arms (where we'd expect more cosmic radiation), which both correspond with the recent icehouse periods on Earth – all consistent with the work of Svensmark and associates on the relation between cosmic radiation and climate through cloud formation. Shaviv and Veizer showed that this could account for most of the large scale temperature changes over the past half billion years (whereas CO_2 was shown to have little effect, if any).

More recently, Shaviv has also shown that records

6. "Evidence for decoupling of atmospheric CO_2 and global climate during the Phanerozoic eon," Ján Veizer, Yves Godderis, Louis M. François, Nature 408, 698-701 (7 December 2000). "Cosmic Ray Diffusion from the Galactic Spiral Arms, Iron Meteorites, and a Possible Climatic Connection?" Physical Review Letters, vol. 89, Issue 5 (2002). Shaviv NJ, Veizer J (2003) Celestial driver of Phanerozoic climate? GSA Today, Geol Soc Am 4–10

FIGURE 8

SOLAR SYSTEM'S MOTION THROUGH SPIRAL ARMS

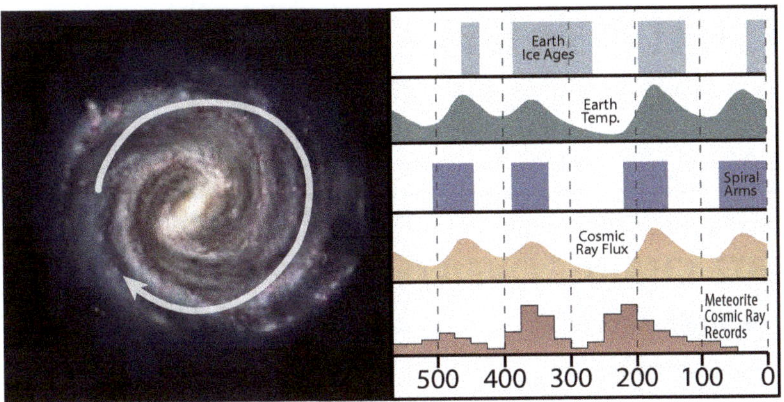

SOLAR SYSTEM'S MOTION THROUGH GALACTIC PLANE

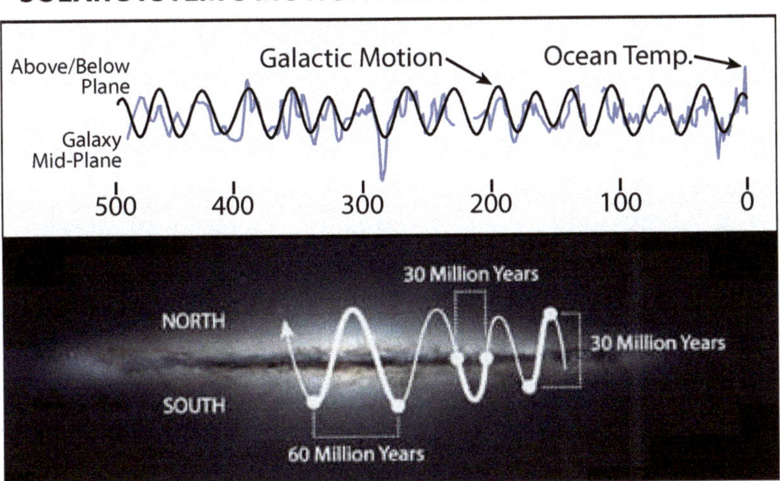

"Is the Solar System's Galactic Motion Imprinted in the Phanerozoic Climate?" Nir J. Shaviv, Andreas Prokoph & Jan Veizer, Nature Science Reports, August 21, 2014; and "The spiral structure of the Milky Way, cosmic rays, and ice age epochs on Earth," by Nir J. Shaviv, New Astronomy 8 (2003) 39–77.

of ocean temperature exhibit a 30 million year periodicity, corresponding to the bobbing motion of our Solar System above and below the plane of our Galaxy. When the Solar System is either above or below the galactic plane the galactic cosmic radiation flux is expected to be less, and ocean records show relatively warmer temperatures (as would be expected from Svensmark's hypothesis); when the Solar System is passing through the galactic plane, galactic cosmic radiation flux is thought to be higher, and ocean records show relatively cooler temperatures (as would be expected from Svensmark's hypothesis). **Figure 8**

Taken together, a growing body of evidence indicates that galactic cosmic radiation plays a major role in affecting climate change (by controlling critical aspects of cloud formation). On shorter timescales of days, to decades, to centuries, to thousands of years, changes in the strength of the Sun's magnetic field regulate the flux of galactic cosmic rays reaching the Earth; and on much longer timescales, tens to hundreds of millions of years, different galactic environments experienced by our Solar System have much larger variations in the density of galactic cosmic radiation. For time periods in between, the most important factor appears to be related to changes in the Earth's orbit and spin axis. Climate change (across all these timescales) is driven by cosmic processes – solar, orbital, and galactic changes – not CO_2.

“Methods” of Climate Alarmists

by Benjamin Deniston

Aug. 3, 2015—Looking at the activity of proponents of the man-made climate change catastrophe narrative, we are left to ask about their apparent methodology – *if the experimental or observational data does not match the model, why not just change the data?*

This brings to mind the statements of some of the founding fathers of the man-made climate change catastrophe scare. Dr. Stephen Schneider, who was one of the early leading advocates of the need to stop a supposed man-made global warming catastrophe in the 1980s (after having warned of an imminent threat of man-made global cooling in the 1970s). Schneider was the founder and editor of the journal Climatic Change, author or co-author of hundreds of papers on climate change, a coordinating lead author in the IPCC's 2001 Third Assessment Report, and a consultant to many US presidential administrations. In a 1989 article in Discover magazine, Schneider was quoted discussing the “method” needed by climate alarmists:

FIGURE 1

CLIMATE CHANGE OVER THE PAST 1,000 YEARS

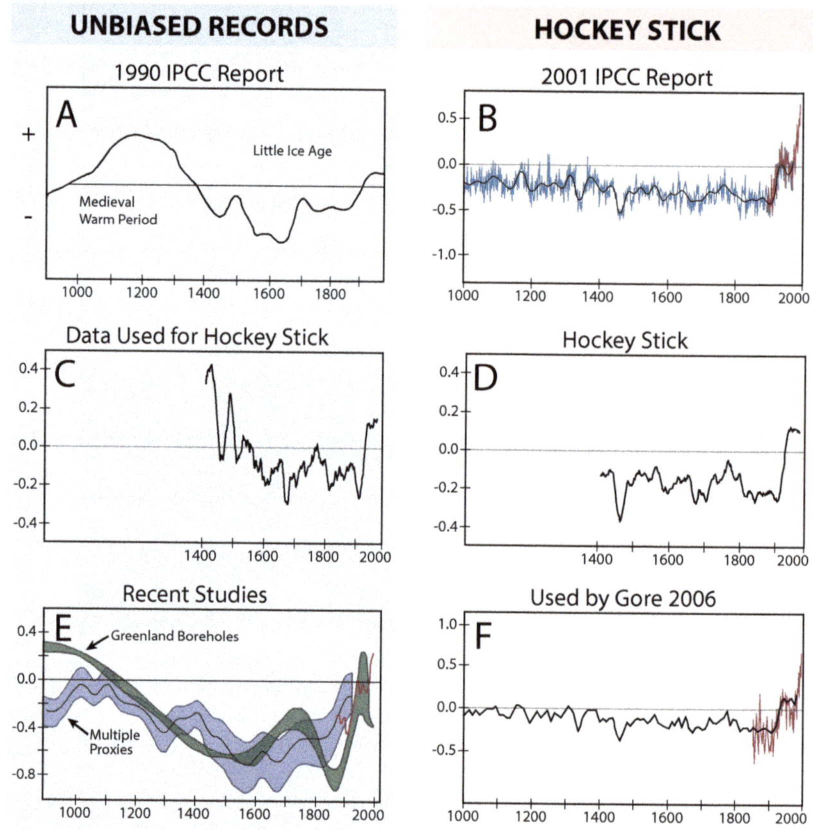

A: featured in the 1990 IPCC report, on the first few pages of Chapter 7, “Observed Climate Variations and Change” as the schematic representation of climate change over the past 1,000 years (page 202). B: 2001 IPCC report. C and D: “Corrections to the Mass et al. (1998) Proxy Data Base and Northern Hemisphere Average Temperature Series,” McIntyre and McKitrick, Energy and Environment, 2003. E: “Cosmic Rays and Climate,” by Jasper Kirkby, Surveys in Geophysics 28, 333–375. F: An Inconvenient Truth.

> On the one hand, as scientists we are ethically bound to the scientific method, in effect promising to tell the truth, the whole truth, and nothing but. … on the other hand, we are not just scientists but human beings as well … we need to get some broad-based support, to capture the public’s imagination. That, of course, entails getting loads of media coverage. So we have to offer up scary scenarios, make simplified, dramatic statements, and make little mention of any doubts we might have… Each of us has to decide what the right balance is between being effective and being honest.[1]

1, S.H. Schneider, In J. Schell “Our Fragile Earth.” Discover (Oct. 1989), pp. 45-48.

FIGURE 2

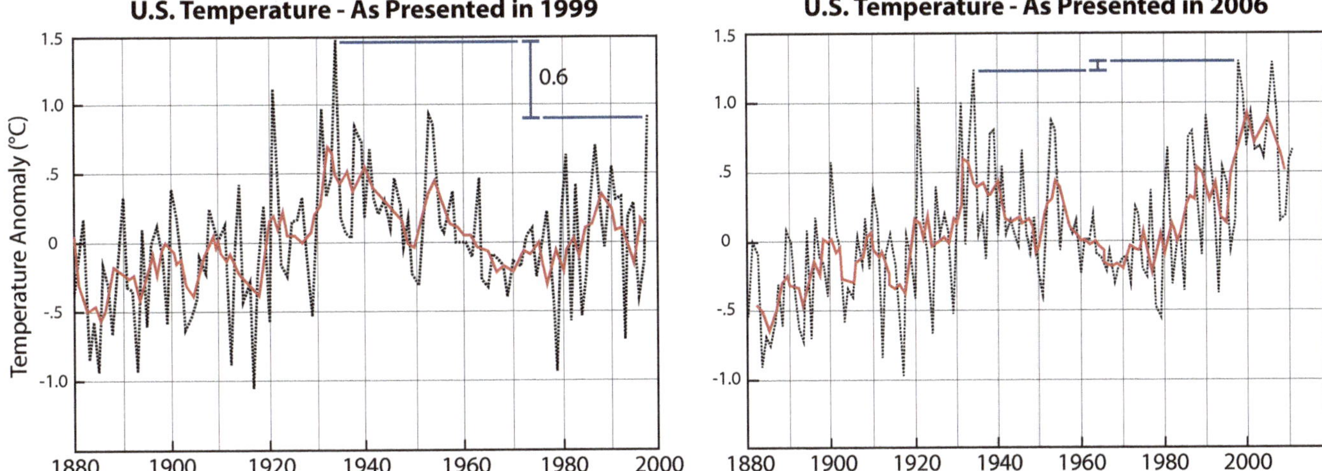

US historical temperature records as of 1999, "Whither U.S. Climate?" James Hansen, Reto Ruedy, Jay Glascoe and Makiko Sato, http://www.giss.nasa.gov/ August 1999.

Dr. Schneider had been a participant in a 1975 "endangered atmosphere" conference organized by Margaret Mead, herself a leading advocate of population reduction.[2] At that conference (which included other soon-to-be leading climate alarmists, including the man who later became Obama's science adviser, John Holdren) Mead used her keynote address to express her promotion of this "method":

> What we need from scientists are estimates, presented with sufficient conservatism and plausibility but at the same time as free as possible from internal disagreements that can be exploited by political interests, that will allow us to start building a system of artificial but effective warnings, warnings which will parallel the instincts of animals who flee before the hurricane, pile up a larger store of nuts before a severe winter, or of caterpillars who respond to impending climatic changes by growing thicker coats.

Recognizing this "methodology" at the roots of the entire movement claiming we're facing imminent catastrophic effects from mankind's CO2 emissions, puts some recent cases of data manipulation and "adjustments" to historical data records in an interesting perspective.

Case 1 – Hockey Stick and Disappearance of the Medieval Warm Period

Much of the narrative that human CO_2 emissions are taking us to a point of catastrophic climate change has been supported by claims that recent warming is "unprecedented." *If* indeed the recent warming had no precedent in recent periods of natural changes, then it would make sense to look for what new (possibly man-made) influence might be causing this deviation from prior natural trends (e.g., recent increases in CO_2 and other emissions).

However many records of past climate have consistently shown that there was a time about 1,000 years ago when temperatures were near current levels, if not warmer. The existence of this "medieval warm period" posed such a challenge to the notion that present warming is "unprecedented," that it was disappeared.

Despite being well recognized enough to be in the IPCC's 1990 First Assessment Report as *the* leading schematic diagram of natural climate change over the past 1,000 years (see **Figure 1**, Box A), by the release of the IPCC's 2001 Third Assessment Report the medieval warm period was conveniently gone. The new presentation of climate change over the past 1,000 years depicted a much flatter and more stable representation of past global temperature, with the only

2. "The Atmosphere: Endangered and Endangering," 1975 conference in Research Triangle Park, North Carolina.

large deviation being a dramatic increase in temperature during the 20th Century (see Figure 1, Box B).

This new presentation of past climate became the go-to illustration to show how "unprecedented" recent climate change has been – proof that mankind must be the factor responsible for this otherwise anomalous deviation from the stable trend of prior centuries.

The only problem with this reassessment of our understanding of the past is that it is ridiculously untrue.

The statistical methods used to produce the new presentation of past global temperature were inherently biased towards producing a flat trend-line followed by a sharp increase – resembling a hockey stick (see Figure 1, Box D). In fact it was shown that if this statistical method was applied to a completely random data set it would produce the same hockey stick effect. When analyzing *the exact same data* with proper methods, the hockey stick character goes away, the medieval warm period returns, and the 20th Century is no longer unprecedented (see Figure 1, Box C).[3]

The IPCC and other alarmists have rejected hundreds of accounts of the medieval warm period in favor of adopting the story presented by a study based on ridiculously dubious methods – *because it fit their desire to "offer up scary scenarios."*

Despite this fraud being revealed by 2003, the hockey stick (or similar depictions) continued to be used, and alarmists continued to claim that recent climate change is unprecedented. For example, Al Gore used a similar depiction in his movie, *An Inconvenient Truth* (see Figure 1, Box F) – a film that was delivered to school teachers across the UK to be used in their curricula.

Recent studies have continued to show the existence of the medieval warm period (see Figure 1, Box E), and while debate continues as to whether it was warmer than the present, the scare-story narrative that the climate change over the past century is unprecedented and dramatically different from historical records is ridiculous.

3. "The Atmosphere: Endangered and Endangering," 1975 conference in Research Triangle Park, North Carolina.

FIGURE 3

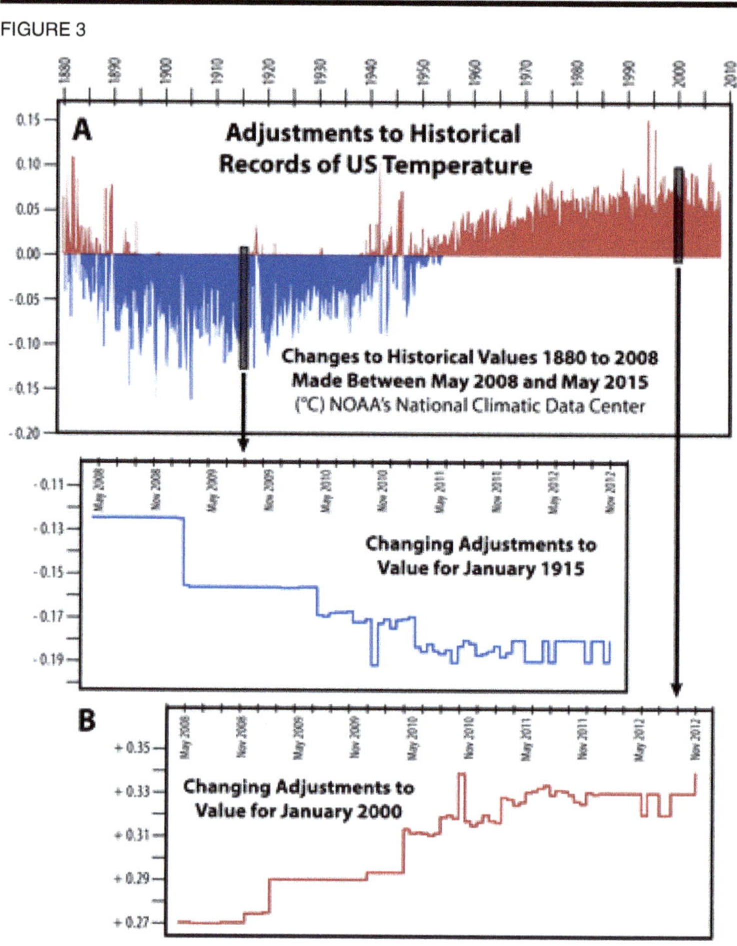

Above, net adjustments to historical records of global temperature between 2008 and 2015, as produced by the US National Climatic Data Center (NCDC). Middle and below, visualization of step by step adjustments for two specific months, January 1915 and January 2000. Image adapted from an original by professor Ole Humlum.

Case 2 – Adjustments of Historical Records and the Elimination of the Pause

It is a difficult challenge to derive a single measure for average global temperature – and not just for past periods (going back thousands or millions of years), but also for recent periods, where we have direct measurements from instruments. Many different measurements – taken in different locations, at different times, and with different instruments – have to be weighted, combined, and averaged in order to provide a single value.

With such an undertaking it is no surprise that prior assessments might get changed and adjusted over time (as methods of analysis might improve or more measurements might become available). However, for those supporting the claim of a coming man-made climate change catastrophe, the adjustments are consistently biased towards supporting their claims. Let's look at a few examples.

When was the hottest period of the past century? The answer to that question would depend upon what region you are talking about, *but it would also depend upon when you asked that question.* For example, in 1999 Dr. James Hansen (then head of the NASA Goddard Institute for Space Studies, which focuses heavily on climate change) authored an article on climate change which utilized a graphic of the official US government assessment of average temperature change in the United States over the past 120 years.[4] By the 1999 figures it was recognized that 1998 was a hot year, but 1921, 1931, 1934, and 1953 were all recorded has hotter years for the United States, with 1934 being over a half a degree (Celsius) hotter (**Figure 2**, Box A).

However, if we examine the records provided by NOAA and NASA today the assessment of temperatures in the past have been adjusted to lower values, with 1921, 1931, 1934, and 1953 all becoming cooler than 1998.

Such convenient adjustments are not limited to the historical records of temperature in the United States. Professor Ole Humlum has analyzed the many adjustments made by the US government's official records of global air surface temperature (produced by NOAA's National Climatic Data Center). Through a series of adjustments between May 2008 and February 2012, the official historical records of global temperature in the first half of the 20th Century have been systematically adjusted cooler, and more recent temperatures systematically adjusted hotter – *accelerating the claimed measured rate of warming solely by adjusting what instrument records were supposed to have said about the past in 2008, versus what the same instrument records were supposed to have said about the past in 2012.*

Figure 3A depicts the cumulative adjustments to the historical global temperatures between 2008 and 2015, and **Figure 3B** analyzes just two specific months, January 1915 and January 2000, examining how the historical values of those two dates changed with each adjustment made between 2008 and 2012.

Most recently, NOAA has released a new revised data set of adjusted global temperatures, leading to new claims of increased warming. Again, this is not showing that the latest data from recent months shows more warming, this is adjusting the assessments from *prior years*, and changing what they claim the past was.

Whereas two assessments of global average temper-

FIGURE 4

GLOBAL TEMPERATURE

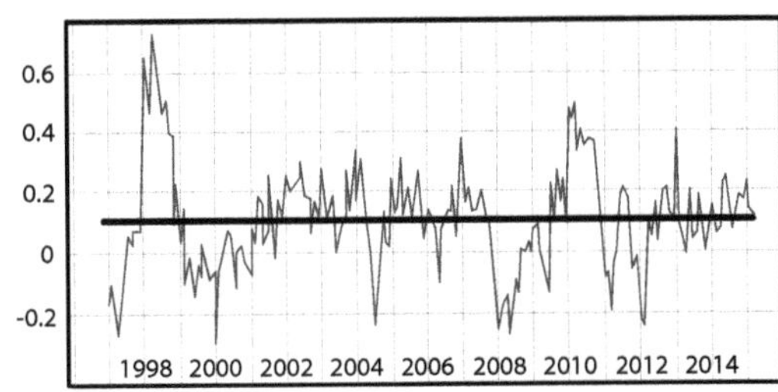

Satellite UAH

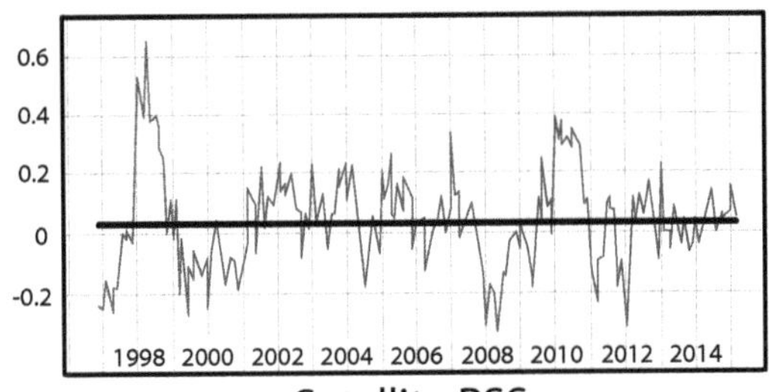

Satellite RSS

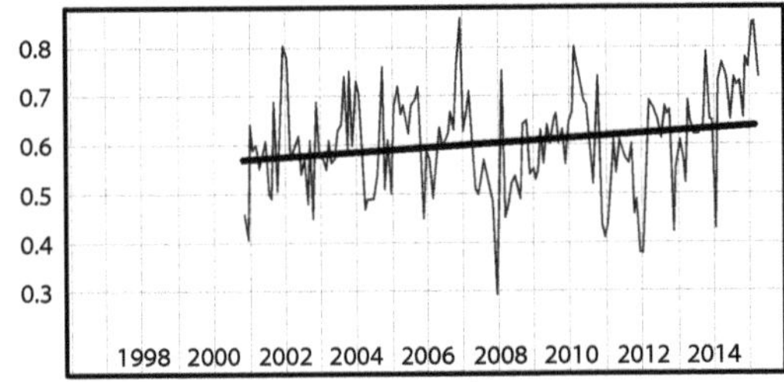

Pre-Adjusted Ground Measurements

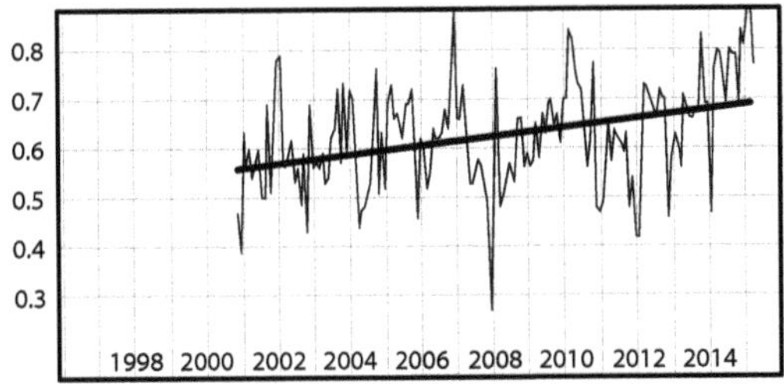

Adjusted Ground Measurements

The RSS (Remote Sensing Systems) and UAH (University of Alabama in Huntsville) analysis of satellite measurements show that there has been no trend of global temperature increase since the late 1990s. Graphics reproduced from originals by Bob Tisdale. Results from adjusted ground measurements from "Possible artifacts of data biases in the recent global surface warming hiatus," Karl et al, Science, June 2015

4. "Whither U.S. Climate?" James Hansen, Reto Ruedy, Jay Glascoe and Makiko Sato, http://www.giss.nasa.gov/ August 1999.

ature based on satellite measurements have shown that global temperatures have not increased for nearly two decades, a new paper utilizing *adjusted* values from NOAA (based on the combination of various land and ocean surface measurements) claims to show that temperatures have been increasing over the past two decades.[5] A section from their abstract reads, "The central estimate for the rate of warming during the first 15 years of the 21st Century is at least as great as the last half of the 20th Century." This flatly contradicts the results provided by two assessments based on satellite measurements, but conveniently fits the narrative of the alarmists.

In one sense, man-made warming is unarguably real: it is created not by CO_2, but rather by "adjusting" the temperature records.

Taken together, these manipulations of past climate records – and the way these manipulations have been used to scare the public – shouldn't be much of a surprise. In the 1970s and 1980s Margaret Mead and Stephen Schneider already told us how the climate alarmists were going to operate, and these more recent data manipulations are just a few examples of their "methods."

---

5. "Possible artifacts of data biases in the recent global surface warming hiatus," Karl et al, Science, June 2015.

III. REJECT 'DECARBONIZATION' FRAUD

Increasing Energy Flux-Density: The Only Competent Energy Policy

by Benjamin Deniston

Some of the earliest archaeological distinctions between mankind and the apes come with the first appearance of ancient fire pits, used to control the power of fire for the betterment of the conditions of life for those wielding that new power.

From that time onward, mankind could no longer be characterized biologically or by biological evolution—the evolution of the creative mental powers unique to the human mind became the determining factor. Biology took a backseat to the increased power of thought wielded by the human species.

Moving to historical times, this secret—and science—of economic growth, can be measured by the control over successively higher forms of fire. This started with transitions to more energy-dense forms of chemical fire, from simple wood burning, to charcoal, then to coal and coke, and onto petroleum and natural gas – one kilogram of coal having 50% more energy than one kilogram of wood, and one kilogram of diesel fuel having 70% more energy than the single kilogram of coal. Each of these new fuels depended upon new chemical reactions, which not only provided the potential for a more energy dense form of fire, but opened up new domains of control and utilization of matter. Metallurgy, materials development, and physical chemistry all developed in dynamic interaction with the development of new forms of fire.

More recently the revolutionary discoveries around the turn of the 20th Century showed mankind an immense potential entirely beyond chemical reactions: Einstein's fundamental equivalence of matter and energy, as expressed in the domains of fission, fusion, and matter-antimatter reactions. Each in this series of relativistic, mass-energy reactions is characterized by successively higher energy densities—and the entire set is orders of magnitude beyond chemical reactions.[1] While this distinction is usefully expressed in the immense difference in the quantity of energy released in nuclear versus chemical reactions – with nuclear reactions having hundreds of thousands to millions of times more energy per mass than chemical reactions – the measured quantitative difference is the effect of a qualitatively distinct, higher domain of action.

Control over higher energy densities enables the increase in what Lyndon LaRouche has defined as the

1. This is why individual nuclear explosives, even small ones, are measured in terms of thousands of tons, or even millions of tons of TNT. The largest thermonuclear weapon ever detonated, the Soviet Union's 1961 Tsar Bomba, was a 50-megaton explosion, meaning it would take the explosion of 50 million tons of TNT to release that much energy from chemical reactions. The Tsar Bomba was a single bomb, dropped from a single airplane (over an unpopulated region of the far north), while 50 million tons of TNT would fill 100 oil supertankers.

TABLE I

The Energy Density of Fuels

FUEL SOURCE	ENERGY DENSITY (J/g)
Combustion Of Wood	1.8 x 104
Combustion Of Coal (Bituminous)	2.7 x 104
Combustion Of Petroleum (Diesel)	4.6 x 104
Combustion Of H2/O2	1.3 x 104 (full mass considered)
Combustion Of H2/O2	1.2 x 105 (only H_2 mass considered)
Typical Nuclear Fuel	3.7 x 109
Direct Fission Energy Of U-235	8.2 x 1010
Deuterium-Tritium Fusion	3.2 x 1011
Annihilation Of Antimatter	9.0 x 1013

Fuel energy densities. The change from wood to matter-antimatter reactions is so great that progress must be counted in orders of magnitude, and the greatest single leap is seen in the transition from chemical to nuclear processes.

FIGURE 1

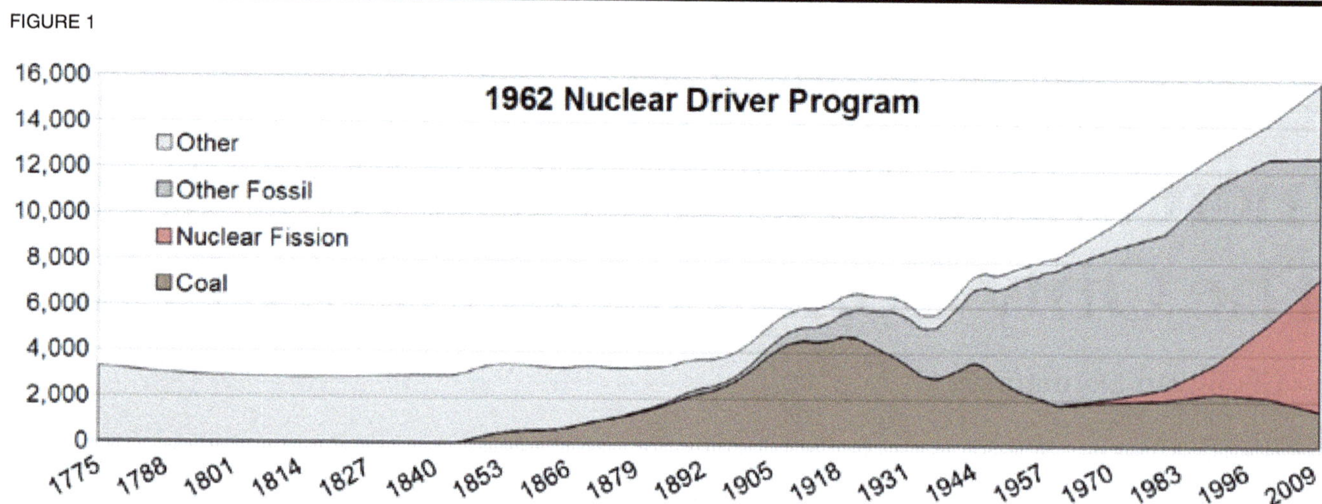

Historical values of watts per capita in the United States, 1775 to 1962, and Glenn Seaborg's Atomic Energy Commission 1962 nuclear power report to President Kennedy projections for 1963 to 2010. Sources, "Civilian Nuclear Power: A Report to the President – 1962," United States Energy Information Administration http://www.eia.gov/

energy flux density of the economy, as can be measured by the rate of energy use per person or per unit area of the economy as a whole. This increasing power is associated with qualitative changes throughout the entire society—fundamentally new technologies, new resource bases, new levels of living standards, and fundamentally new economies.

On the contrary, so-called green energy sources represent a step *backwards*. Much lower levels of energy provided per physical economic cost, and notoriously unreliable and sporadic generation, mean that large-scale implementation of wind and solar power *lowers* the national economic energy flux-density, as is most starkly being demonstrated in Germany presently. (See "Germany: Case Study in the Failure of Green Energy".)

Both these trends – the qualitative progress associated with increasing energy flux-density, and the negative effects of a green policy – have been expressed in the history of the United States.

National Economic Energy Flux-Density: USA Case Study

Start with the simple rate of biological energy usage for the human body, which is, very roughly, 100 watts (corresponding to consuming 2,000 food calories a day). Assuming a hypothetical pre-fire civilization in which all work is performed by human muscle, the power employed to sustain this society is 100 watts per capita .

Compare this with the changing per capita power usage throughout the history of the United States.

At the time of the United States' founding, the wood-based economy provided around 3,000 watts per capita. This does not mean every individual used 3,000 watts; it includes all the power supplied to agriculture, industry, and other areas *supporting the economy as a whole*, averaged to a per capita value. In this wood-based economy, the effective power that each individual wielded and represented (expressed in terms of the individual's relation to the unity of the national economic system as a whole) was thirty times higher than the simple muscle power of a hypothetical fire-less society. This was not just "more" energy, but a quality of energy that enabled people to create states of matter and chemistry which could never be created by muscle power alone (exemplified by advances in metallurgy, for example, creating the basis for new tools, machinery, and other technologies).

The increasing use of coal throughout the economy raised the power to over 5,000 watts per capita by the 1920s. Each individual then expressed nearly twice the power of the wood-based economy (again, expressed in terms of the individual's relation to the entire national economy), supporting the motion-producing, heat-powered machinery and transportation which revolutionized the industrialized economy. The development of modern chemistry enabled the beginnings of a new revolution in mankind's understanding of and control over matter.

By the early 1960s the use of petroleum and natural gas had brought power to over 8,000 watts per capita – 80 times the per capita power of our hypothetical fire-less society – and nuclear fission power was fully ca-

FIGURE 2

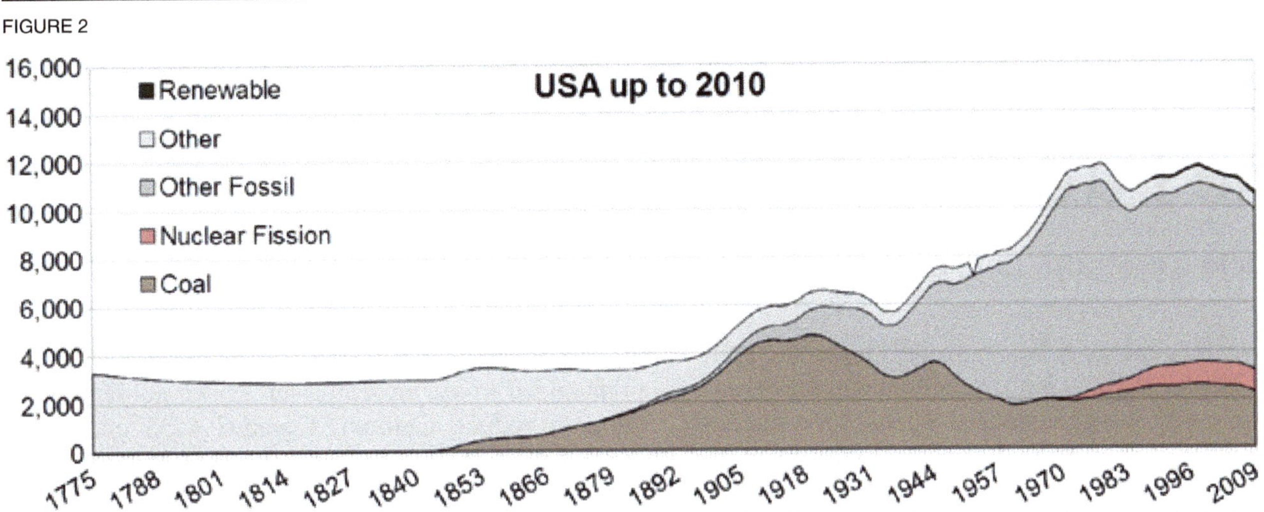

Watts per capita throughout the history of the United States, 1775 to 2010. The renewable category includes wind, solar, geothermal, and biofuels (but not hydroelectric power). Source, the United States Energy Information Administration http://www.eia.gov/

pable of sustaining the U.S. historical growth rate well into the 21st Century.

In 1962 President John F. Kennedy commissioned his Atomic Energy Commission – then under the direction of Glenn Seaborg – to "take a new and hard look at the role of nuclear power in our economy." Seaborg's 70-page report, released that year, outlined a transition consistent with prior transitions from lower to higher energy sources: coal use leveling off and declining by the turn of the century, with nuclear power becoming the dominant electricity source for the nation. By Seaborg's forecast, this nuclear driver program would have brought the national economic energy flux-density to nearly 16,000 watts per capita by 2010.

By then, assuming the nation had maintained a pro-growth orientation, as fission power was becoming the dominant power source, the beginnings of applied fusion power should have begun to emerge. With isotopes of hydrogen and helium as an effectively limitless fuel source for fusion reactors, the U.S. economy would be on a path to even higher levels energy flux density – continuing this process of limitless progress. Virtually every concern over resource limitations (from food, to water, to metals, etc.) and energy limitations for all mankind, across the entire planet, can be addressed with a fusion economy—and that, for countless generations to come.

However, in the United States this natural growth process was cut off by the zero-growth policies of the green movement.

The green policy locked the economy on a path into the attritional collapse being experienced now—a collapse process accelerated by policies which lower the energy flux density of the economy. Nuclear fission power was never allowed to realize its full potential; instead, there was an increasing emphasis on solar, wind, and other forms of green energy, and the energy flux-density of the economy stagnated, and began to collapse.

This brought degenerative effects. Instead of the per capita use of coal continuing to decline (in a natural transition to nuclear power), it began to increase again by the late 1970s. Under the green, zero-growth paradigm, per capita coal use in 2010 was 33% higher than it would have been under Seaborg's nuclear driver proposal to Kennedy – with the total national energy flux-density 33% lower than it would have been under the nuclear driver program.

The 40-year gap between the expected natural growth of a progressing economy and present levels of stagnation and decline under a green policy is a measure of the current economic breakdown of the United States, and demonstrates the immediate need for a crash program to develop and implement the next stage, the fusion economy, to overcome decades of lost time and accumulated attrition by creating a new economy at a higher level than ever before.

So-called green technologies will not work (as Germany is now showing to the world). Increasing qualities of power—of "fire"—is the essential characteristic of mankind, measuring our success in satisfying the need for continual progress.

Germany: Case Study in The Failure of Green Energy

by Alicia Cerretani, Benjamin Deniston

Germany's energy policy, especially under the influence of Hans Joachim (John) Schellnhuber, serves as a warning: green energy is not sustainable for a modern industrial economy. Germany's nuclear exit – with laws established to fully eliminate nuclear power in Germany by 2022 – coupled with its massive expansion of solar and wind, has been a disaster. Since this policy has been aggressively implemented for some years, we can now examine the results.

In 2013 an author for the leftist {Dissent} magazine provided a breakdown of the realities of wind and solar power in Germany in 2012:[1]

In 2012 German wind power advertised an installed electrical generation capacity of nearly 31,000 megawatts, but the average production for the year *was only 17% of that capacity*. Solar power fared even worse: with an advertised capacity of 29,000 megawatts, its average generation for the year was only *11% of capacity*.

The expansion of inefficient wind and solar has been massively subsidized, and the costs of electricity are so high that people in Germany call their energy bill their "second mortgage." In 2004 residential electricity was about 23 cents (U.S.) per kilowatt-hour, and by 2015 it was 35 cents (among the highest prices for any developed nation); electricity prices for companies have risen 60% over the past five years, driving Germany's critical industrial and manufacturing out of the nation. A significant portion of this cost increase is directly from a "renewable energy surcharge" added to electricity bills to cover the cost of key subsidies to wind and solar. In 2013 German renewable energy subsidies were around 27 billion US dollars,[2] adding seven cents per kilowatt-hour to electricity bills – an added green energy surcharge which, alone, was nearly 70% of the average total electricity rate in the United States. In an added irony, these measures have not done anything to reduce Germany's annual CO2 emissions, which have remained the same for the past decade.

At the Tenth International Conference on Climate Change (held in Washington D.C., 2015) an overview of the failure of Germany's wind and solar power program was presented by Wolfgang Müller (the General Secretary of the European Institute for Climate and Energy), providing further details of Germany's failed energy policy.[3]

Wind

Between 1994 and 2012, the number of wind turbines in Germany increased from roughly 2,000 to 23,000. Not only do they operate far below capacity, the output fluctuates wildly. In 2014 Germany's 35,000 megawatts of wind power capacity operates at less than 30% of capacity 90% of the time, and at less than 10% of capacity 55% of the time (never reaching above 70%).

To illustrate the dramatically varying, and often minimal, production of power from wind we can examine data from a single month of electricity generation (August 2014) in Figure 1.

Solar

In 2000 Germany solar power capacity was merely 114 megawatts. In 15 years' time – driven by their massive subsidy program – this was increased over 300-fold, to 37,400 megawatts. As with wind, the actual electricity generation never comes close to this advertised capacity figure, and output varies significantly – reaching over 40% of capacity only 11% of the time, and remaining below 30% of capacity 60% of the time.

The fluctuation is not merely from the obvious day-night variation, but day to day as well, with power pro-

1. "Green Energy Bust in Germany," by Will Boisvert, Dissent, Summer 2013.

2. More than the United States government has spent on funding magnetic confinement fusion research over the past 50 years.

3. Tenth International Conference on Climate Change (ICCC), Panel 5: "Climate Program Impacts," Heartland Institute, June 11, 2015.

FIGURE 1
Wind: Installed Capacity vs. Output
Maximum installed capacity=35,000 MW

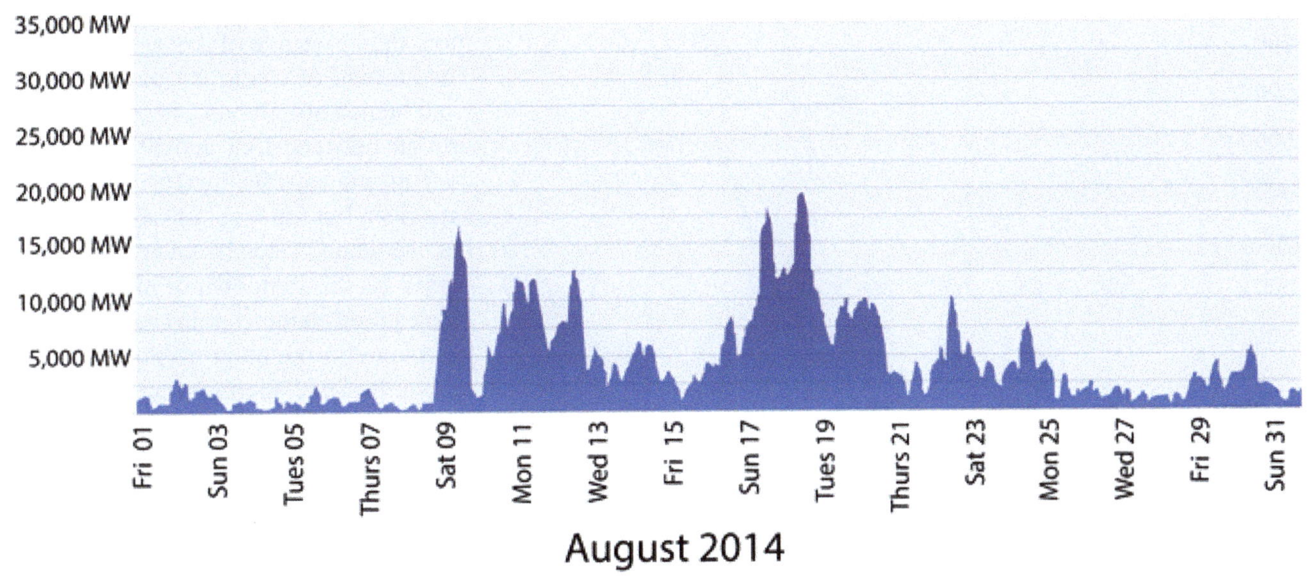

Electricity generated from all of Germany's wind turbines during the month of August 2014, measured against the advertised installed capacity. Image adapted from that used by Wolfgang Müller at the 2015 ICCC.

FIGURE 2
PV: Installed Capacity vs. Output
Maximum installed capacity=37,400 MW

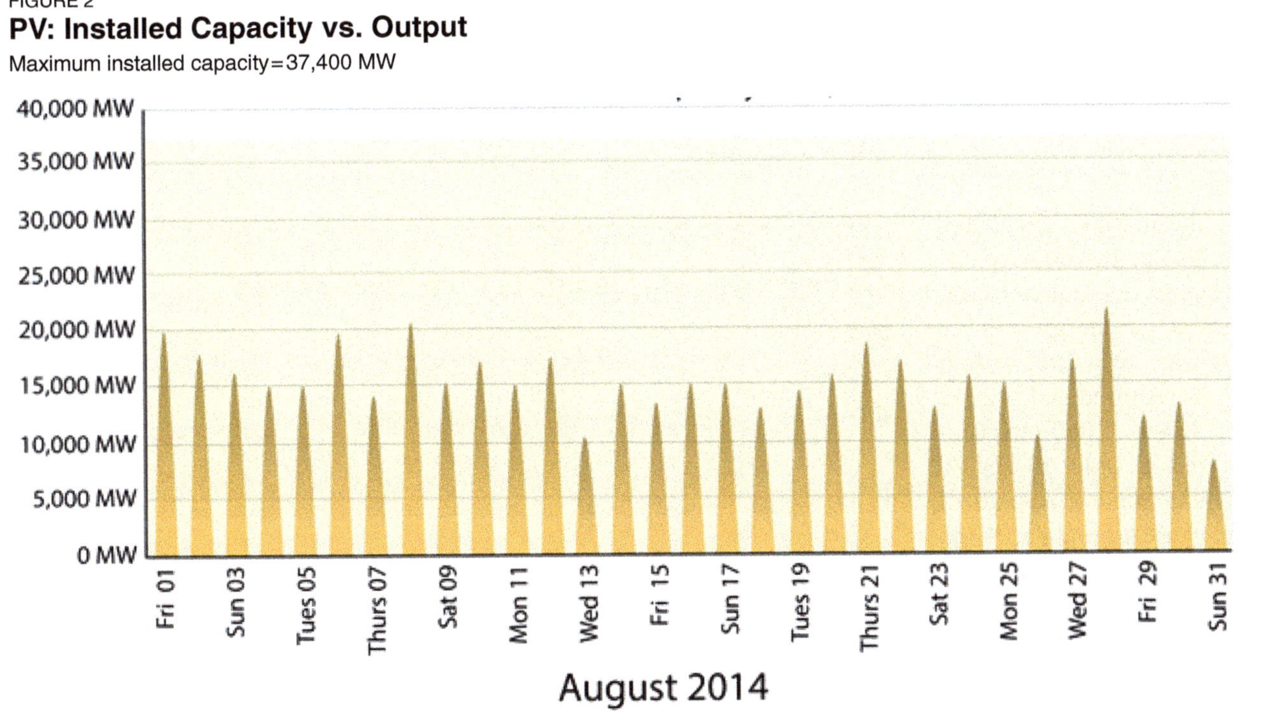

Electricity generated from all of German solar power during the month of August 2014, measured against the advertised installed capacity. Image adapted from that used by Wolfgang Müller at the 2015 ICCC.

FIGURE 3

Interventions To Stabilize the Grid

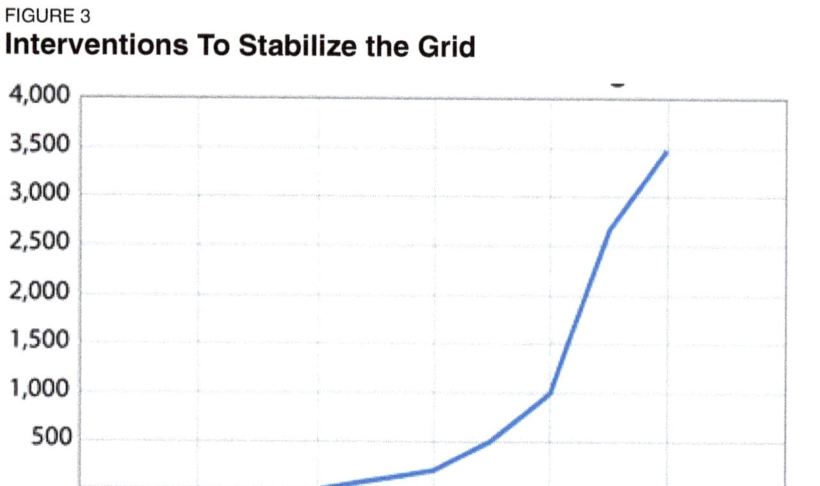

Number of interventions required to stabilize the electrical grid in Germany, 2004 to 2014. Image adapted from that used by Wolfgang Müller at the 2015 ICCC.

duction at the mercy of the clouds. A more detailed examination of a single month shows the dramatic fluctuation in the electricity generation in Figure 2.

Problems for the Grid

If we take Germany's wind and solar power together in 2014, 75% of the time they operated below 20% of their cumulative installed capacity, and the irregular starts and stops created problems for an electrical delivery grid which depends upon reliable supplies of power.

Before the massive expansion of wind and solar power, very few interventions were required to stabilize Germany's energy grid. In 2006 there were only three or four interventions required, but in 2012 there were nearly 1,000 interventions required in order to keep a consistent and reliable source of energy available around the clock. In 2014 over 3,500 such interventions were required to rescue the national energy supply from the effects of fluctuations due to unreliable supply inputs. The trend is shown in **Figure 3**.

As an added irony to the whole insanity which has been Germany's energy policy under Chancellor Angela Merkel and John Schellnhuber, Germany's level of CO2 emissions has not changed after more than a decade of this green program. The amount of electricity put on the grid from "renewable" sources has nearly quadrupled between 2000 and 2013 (requiring over an eleven-fold increase in installed capacity), but the level of CO2 emissions has remained steady over that entire period, as the shutdown of nuclear power has required an increase in coal and natural gas plants to maintain stable power supplies. In 2012 Germany commissioned 2,900 megawatts of new coal power plants, capable of providing nearly twice the power of all the wind and solar added in that same year.

In total, Germany has massively subsidized a monstrous expansion of inefficient green energy supplies, providing irregular and sporadic power, creating a physical economic drain on the German economy, driving out productive industry and manufacturing, without producing the slightest reduction in their CO2 emissions – and at the price of a "second mortgage" to Germans in the form of their electricity bill.

Let the lesson be learned – there is no need for other nations to repeat this failure.

FIGURE 4

CO_2 Emissions vs. Electricity from 'Renewables'

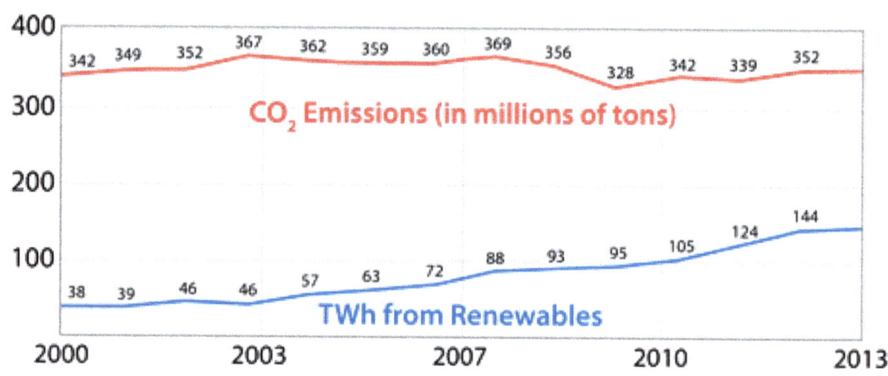

Electricity produced from renewable sources in Germany compared with total CO2 emissions; despite a nearly four-fold increase in renewable energy, there is no decrease in CO2 emissions. Image adapted from that used by Wolfgang Müller at the 2015 ICCC

The Facts on Fusion

by Liona Fan-Chiang, Benjamin Deniston

When mentioning fusion power the refrain, "fusion is *always* 30 years away," has become a recurring bad joke. While this cynical statement is often presented as a supposed proof that fusion has practically insurmountable technical challenges, the reality is quite different.

In 1976 the United States Energy Research and Development Administration (a precursor to the modern US Department of Energy) published a thorough roadmap to reach fusion power, "Fusion Power by Magnetic Confinement Program Plan" (ERDA 76-110). Under the direction of Dr. Stephen Dean, the 1976 report proposed a dynamic roadmap, with various reactor designs, stages, and goals which were to be pursued in order to reach the development of a functioning first generation fusion power plant (which was to be commercializable for the development and implementation of second generation systems throughout the economy).

FIGURE 1

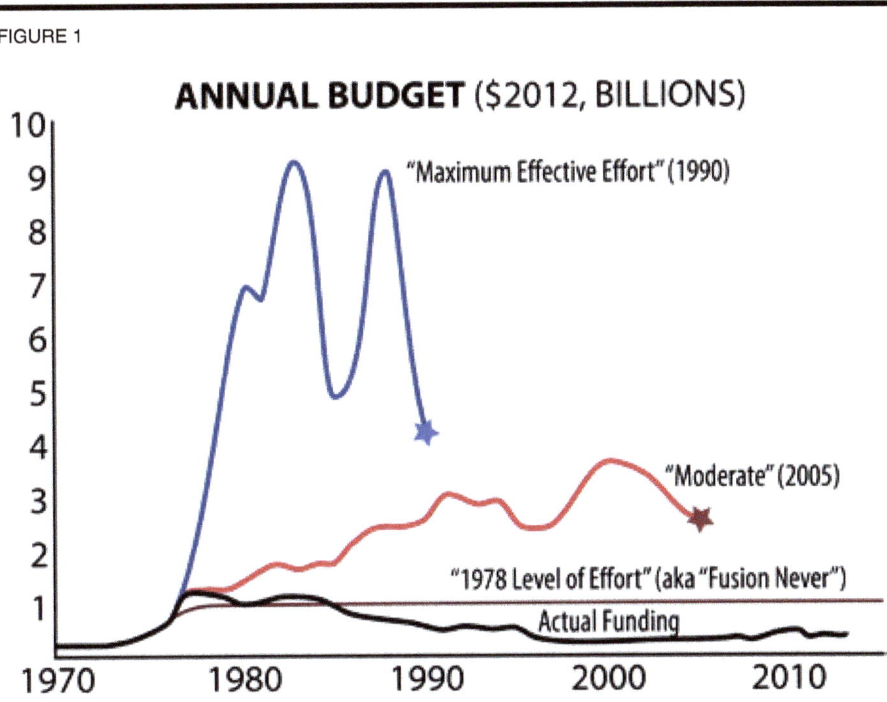

Possible paths to fusion power from 1976 according to the 1976 "Fusion Power by Magnetic Confinement Program Plan" of the Energy Research and Development Administration, compared with actual funding levels for magnetic confinement fusion. Annual budget measured in billions of dollars (2012 dollars). Graphic adapted from original by Geoff Olynyk

According to the lengthy and detailed 1976 plan, the speed by which the different stages would be reached – and the final date of achieving a functioning fusion power plant – *was wholly dependent upon the level of funding provided.* With an accelerated crash effort, supported by an annual budget ranging from $4 to $9 billion (in 2012 dollars), fusion power was projected to be achievable by 1990. With a more moderate approach, supported by an annual budget ranging from $2 to $4 billion, fusion power was to be brought online by 2005.[1]

Why don't we have fusion power today? Why do people say fusion is still "30 years away"? *Because the level of funding which was known to have been required was simply never provided.* The actual funding has not only been far below the "moderate" path, *it has been well below a level which was already known to be too little to ensure fusion power would ever be reached.* (See **Figure 1**.)

1. For comparison, in 2013 alone Germany provided $27 billion in subsidies to "renewable" energy, led by solar and wind power.

In short, the United States doesn't have fusion power because the government has followed a policy *not* to develop fusion power.

10 to 15 Years Away

What if the United States decided to make a crash effort to develop fusion power? Independent sources have provided similar assessments: it would take between 10 and 15 years to develop a functioning first-generation fusion power reactor, if the proper level of funding and qualified support were provided.

Dr. Stephen Dean: 15 Years – In the mid-1960s Dr. Dean co-authored the Atomic Energy Commission's Policy for Controlled Thermonuclear Research; in 1976 he headed the development of the Energy Research and Development Administration's report "Fusion Power by Magnetic Confinement Program Plan;" and since 1979 he has served as the president of the non-profit foundation Fusion Power Associates (an organization which continues to regularly bring together leading fusion scientists from around the world in an effort to promote the development of fusion power). Following five decades of high level experience, Dr. Dean is extremely well positioned to be able to provide a qualified assessment of how long it would take to bring fusion power online, if the proper support were given. In discussions with *21st Century Science and Technology* in 2014, Dr. Dean expressed that he thought it could be done in 15 years, under a true crash program.

Lyndon LaRouche: 10 to 15 Years – Lyndon LaRouche was in the center of the fight for fusion power throughout the 1970s and 1980s, having been the founder of the Fusion Energy Foundation, *Fusion* magazine, and the *International Journal of Fusion Energy*. These publications and institutions provided a forum for collaboration among leading fusion scientists, engineers, and policy makers from around the world – including through dozens of international conferences and seminars – building widespread political and popular support for the development of fusion power. Through discussions with contacts in and around the institutions of the United States presidency over the recent few years, LaRouche has agreed that a 10 to 15 year time frame to achieve fusion power is feasible – if the proper support is provided.

American Security Project: 10 Years – The American Security Project is an organization run by an array of high-level representatives from military, intelligence, political, and industrial backgrounds. Based on their concern for energy independence and security for the United States, they have coordinated their own assessment of the time and effort required to bring fusion power online. As presented in their 2013 white paper, "Fusion Power – A 10 Year Plan to Energy Security," they have also concluded that a one-decade crash program is a feasible timeframe.

International Progress

Even without a crash effort, progress is being made on various national and international fronts, with Asian nations quickly accelerating their efforts. While there are no set dates for the construction of a fully functioning fusion power plant – yet – an array of leading research reactors are making important steps (even under major funding constraints).

The International Thermonuclear Experimental Reactor (ITER) is a tokamak fusion reactor being built in France through a joint effort between the European Union, India, Japan, China, Russia, South Korea and the United States. With plans to produce 500 megawatts of power from only 50 megawatts power input, this will be an important step in the progress towards fusion power (even though no electricity will be generated from the fusion reactions). Unfortunately, funding limitations and delays have extended the construction time and cost of the project – with plans for first plasma generation in the early 2020s, and full operations in the late 2020s. It is important to emphasize that, while ITER will have more advanced electronics and engineering, the basic design and goals could have been achieved *in the 1980s* (had the effort been made at the time).

ITER's operations will be a complementary advance upon existing experimental reactors. Nations in Europe, the United States, China, South Korea, Japan, and India (among others) all have advanced experimental fusion reactors, testing and demonstrating critical engineering and science objectives needed for fusion power.

However, certain nations are placing an increasing focus on advancing their own programs at a faster rate. With South Korea, China, and India making rapid progress, it is entirely possible that the first fully operational fusion power plant will be built and operated in Asia.

A Surge of Private Efforts

The feasibility and importance of fusion power is also being underscored by the past decade's surge in private initiatives to develop commercialized fusion power. Many of the designs being pursued by private companies are modifications or combinations of older operational designs which had been investigated by government programs early on (including in the 1976 Project Plan referenced above), but were never funded or developed (despite having many promising features).

The large aerospace company Lockheed Martin is working on a compact fusion reactor through their research and development outfit Skunk Works. While their ambitious timeframe has been questioned by some, they are working towards a 2017 completion date for a prototype 100 megawatt fusion reactor, to be followed by a power plant prototype (able to generate electricity) five years later.

In another effort, a stealth company based in California, Tri Alpha Energy, has generated diverse international investment for the development of its own designs for a fusion reactor, with plans of developing a 100 megawatt power plant. As of 2014, the company said it employed over 150 people and had raised more than $140 million for their fusion efforts.

A Canadian company, General Fusion, has said they are working towards a fusion reactor by 2020. With investments from venture capital and the Canadian government, the company had raised $55 million for their efforts by 2013.

In New Jersey the company Lawrenceville Plasma Physics is working on the development of their Focus Fusion system. Their goal is a smaller system, capable of providing 5 megawatts of power at a cost of 0.3 cents per kilowatt hour (less than a tenth of electricity costs in the United States).

Fusion is the Future

Despite the lack of support and extensive delays, fusion power is within reach.

Not only will a fusion economy provide an effectively limitless energy supply, but it will open up entirely new types of industries, enable new methods of production, and make accessible entirely new natural resource bases. Just as the discovery of charcoal production and metallurgy changed mineral deposits into valuable resources, creating the bronze and iron ages, and the perfection of internal combustion engines made oil a critical economic resource, so too will fusion transform our relation to the physical chemistry of our planet, and beyond. In addition to cheap electricity, making all the current functions of economy physically easier, it will unlock dramatically different processes of materials-processing, manufacturing, and space-propulsion. As chemistry has made use of the electron-related properties of atoms, with nuclear science we stand poised to avail ourselves of the new physical forces discovered in the atomic nucleus, such as the "strong force," whose name suggests the 1,000,000-times increase in the power of nuclear reactions, compared to chemical (atomic) ones.

This is the necessary next step for mankind's progress, as measured by increasing levels of energy flux-density.

Wall Street and London Made a 'Carbon Copy' of the Subprime Swindle

by Paul Gallagher

July 28, 2015—Deutsche Bank, the world's largest bank for financial derivatives, erected a 70-foot-tall doomsday "carbon clock" in New York City's Madison Square Garden in 2011, tracking greenhouse-gas emission levels in real time: 2 billion metric tons added each month, or 800 tonnes a second.

The garish display was, in fact, part of another Deutsche Bank financial fraud, carried out by traders on the bank's carbon trading floor in Frankfurt, Germany. In May 2015, Frankfurt's chief prosecutor announced an ongoing investigation of 26 current or former carbon-emissions traders at Deutsche Bank—17 on suspicion of tax evasion, five for money laundering and four for obstruction of justice—all in connection with the European Union's carbon trading network and the United Nations' so-called Clean Development Mechanism. On July 15, eight were arrested and charged with tax evasion in connection with carbon trading. The Frankfurt prosecutor accuses them of securing fees and bonuses from participating in a "carbon emission certificate" scam that resulted in tax evasion worth 136 million euros ($149 million), the magazine reported.

At least 14 people from two banks have been jailed in three countries so far, for their involvement in carbon trading tax fraud. The European police agency Europol has estimated such crime has cost taxpayers more than 5 billion euros in lost revenue since 2008. The repeated raids at Deutsche Bank over carbon-trading fraud in the past two years contributed to the resignations of the bank's co-CEOs in June.

"Decarbonization of the world economy," as proposed by the British Royal Family satanic advisors like John Schellnhuber, is not only a genocidal proposal, impossible without killing billions of people. It has also been seized on by big banks and big oil as the justification for creating a new derivatives, or "swaps" bubble from which they can make large profits and fees while holding back growth and development in industrializing countries.

Fees for Delivering Nothing to No One

At the big annual United Nations "climate conferences"—in Copenhagen in 2009, Warsaw in 2013, Durban in 2012, scheduled for Paris this December—the biggest delegations are not scientists or environmental activists, but "suits" from the International Emissions Trading Association. The IETA is made up of major international banks led by Goldman Sachs, JPMorgan Chase, Bank of America, the biggest oil and raw materials extraction companies like BP, Shell, Total, Anglo-American Corp., BHP Billiton, Rio Tinto, Glencore Xstrata, etc.; and the carbon trading companies they have created, like EDF Trading.

Carbon "cap-and-trade" is the IETA's invention, specifically designed for the European carbon emissions market (the world's largest) by BP Chairman Peter Sutherland in 2006. While still chairman at that great Gulf of Mexico polluter, Sutherland became special advisor to European Commission head José Manuel Barroso to design the EU Emissions Trading System, or EU ETS.

Carbon emissions trading precisely mirrors trading in mortgage-backed securities and CLO and CDO derivatives in the real estate bubble while imploded in 2007; but in fact, it makes that bubble look transparent by comparison. In carbon emissions trading, the "underlying product" literally is not supposed to exist. To quote one published analysis from 2010, "The carbon market is based on the lack of delivery of an invisible substance to no one."

But this fee-generating phantasm had become in 2012, "the world's fastest growing commodities market" according to the World Bank (which prioritizes it over infrastructure in its financing) valued at about $176 billion in 2011. The EU ETS dominated with $148 billion "value".

Since 2011 this "fastest-growing market" has become a mass of tax evasion, securities fraud, money-laundering and other crimes as exemplified by the trading. As Blue Source stated in *MIT Technology Review*, "Blue Source's project is innovative not technically—the company employs off-the-shelf technology—but financially: It is among the first whose business plan hinges on the sale of both the captured carbon dioxide and carbon offsets, a financial derivative generated from the emissions reduction."

Creative Commons/Sebastian Schlüter

What carbon trading hath wrought in skies of Europe: In August 2012, German Environment Minister Peter Altmaier said the country would need to build more coal-fired power plants to ensure energy supplies, "even as Germany is pursuing one of the world's most ambitious climate protection strategies."

Deutsche Bank traders, and a source of superprofits for some large companies which, ironically, are considered to be "industrial polluters." The U.S.-based carbon trading market CCX, set up in Chicago in 2007 as a carbon copy of the EU ETS—by Goldman Sachs and Dr. Richard Sandor of the London International Financial Futures Exchange (inventor of the collateralized mortgage obligation!)—has collapsed and been shut down. But one of Goldman-Sachs' legal exploitations of carbon trading can be taken as an example.

The Goldman-controlled Utah-based company Blue Source built a small pipeline network to ship carbon dioxide exit gas from a natural gas plant in Colorado, to shale oil fracking companies. Since Blue Source was not venting the invisible CO2 into the air at the gas plant (it was venting methane instead), it got "emissions credits" for that nothing from the EU ETS, and sold *them* to "polluters," in the United States or Europe, including some of the same shale drilling companies! Meanwhile those companies were mixing the CO2 with water and chemicals to make "fracking water" for high-pressure pumping into aging oil seams—a waste of water, a source of water pollution, a highly inefficient oil production method, and apparently a cause of earthquakes if done intensively in a state.

The result was double profits for Blue Source and Goldman Sachs, which also earned fees on the carbon trading.

Stopping Development

But in half of all trades on this market, the "product" has been something proposed *not to happen* in a developing country—farmland not being cleared, electricity not being produced or roads or railroads not being built, areas being locked away against development—and the "trade" has been the ability of multinationals and other major corporations to emit more carbon dioxide, methane, or other compounds.

This half is trading in the emissions permits of the United Nations' so-called Clean Development Mechanism, and here all aspects of the mortgage-backed securities/derivatives bubbles ca. 2005 are reproduced. The UN accredits four major standards companies as "ratings agencies," which it calls Designated Operational Entities or DOEs. The major banks and multinationals employ "carbon developers" who look for supposed carbon dioxide-saving projects in developing countries—*not* clearing or tilling land, planting trees, composting waste for fertilizer in a way which supposedly releases less methane than is "customary," etc.—on which they can "issue securities." The major banks and multis employing these "carbon developers" also pay the UN-approved DOEs or "ratings agencies" to accredit carbon emission "savings" over some period of years. The DOE's have generally approved over 90% of the proposals. Then the UN issues emissions credits to, say, Anglo-American Corp; those credits become the securities which are traded, with derivatives being issued on them, for years, while the UN is waiting to see if any carbon emissions are actually saved. If the project does not make any difference, or if the developer trades the credit for 10 years and then cuts the trees down anyway, the UN does not collect any refunds or fines!

And the final touch: emissions assessors, after working for the DOEs or "ratings agencies" for a few years, typically try to get jobs as "carbon developers" or on the carbon-trading desks of banks.

Of the four DOE companies, two have been suspended by the UN for shoddy standards—Norway's Det Norske Veritas (DNV) and the French SGS Group weights-and-measures firm. The UN has approved more than 2,000 "projects" for 300 million emissions credits, "worth" tens of billions of dollars as securities on the carbon-trading market with their futures and derivatives nominally worth much more—until it collapsed.

'Polluters' Make Eco-Profits

In the *Laudato Si'* encyclical in which Pope Francis bought into the satanic Gaia worship of "Mother Earth," the many pages of simplistic railing against "pollution" showed the Pontifical Academy of Sciences abandoning all knowledge of the relation of human technology to the biosphere. The Pope would be in for a nasty surprise, to learn that the "worldwide decarbonization" schemes of British royal advisors are implemented by "carbon trading" in which "pollution" is profitable, and "more pollution" is more profitable.

The European Union half of the carbon-trading market—the EU ETS named above—was originally designed by British Lord Nicholas Stern. Every year since it began in 2004, the European governments, through the ETS, have given out to the oil, steel, coal, chemicals, electricity, agriculture and other sectors, emissions credits or allowances equal to 10% or so *more* than the total tonnage of carbon dioxide, methane, sulfur dioxide, etc. that sector had emitted the year before. Big companies whose emissions went over the allowance they'd received were supposed to buy "emissions credits" from others through dealers on the EU ETS carbon exchange; but in fact, they didn't have to. Instead, companies and banks speculated on futures and derivatives of their emissions credits, waiting to use them in the future. Or, in the case of the big electricity producers, for example, they added a lot of coal-fired electricity plants—importing coal from the United States—and collected emissions credits for putting modern scrubbers on the stacks: standard technology which they would have used anyway!

In 2009, an *Engineering and Technology Magazine* analyst was carried away enough to write: "The continued spectacular growth of the carbon markets shows no sign of holding back. From 22bn [euros] in 2006, to 40bn in 2007 and to an estimated 100bn in 2008. By some estimates, that figure could rise to 550bn by 2012 and, with the inclusion of the U.S., 3tr in 2020."

But, "At the same time, you cannot help but notice that man-made carbon emissions are still going up; in the 1990s by 0.8 per cent per year, rising to 3.1 per cent from 2000 to 2006. In other words, a nearly 40 per cent increase from 6.2bn tonnes in 1990 to 8.5bn tonnes in 2007."

In 2013 Trans-National Institute produced a report on Anglo-American Corp.'s fraudulent use of carbon emission certificates to increase the profitability of its mining activities in Colombia, with no changes in technology, productivity, or efficiency. "Since its inception," TNI wrote, the ETS [EU Emission Trading System]'s permeability to industry lobbyists has ensured it is so full of loopholes that polluters can avoid making any domestic emissions reductions.... The free and excessive numbers of emissions allowances have enabled polluters to make billions of euros of windfall profits, in some case scandalously passing on the costs of the allowances to consumers, as if they had been paid for."

Electricity producer RWE, Europe's largest industrial source of carbon dioxide, made $6.4 billion extra profits on the carbon-trading markets in 2009-2011, as documented in the 2015 book *Eco-Hustle!* by Bruce E. Johansen Ph.D. Companies throughout the 30 countries of the ETS made $374 billion extra profits in that period, Dr. Johansen shows. Companies building wind-turbine or solar-panel "farms" were able both to collect government subsidies and sell emissions credits on the ETS; in addition, they collected the value-added tax on the credits, which they may or may not have remitted to the governments. The Deutsche Bank traders arrested July 25 did not.

After the 2008 financial crash, as economic activity and demand for commodities fell, the over-issue of emissions credits became more exaggerated, until the carbon trading market largely collapsed. The price of a credit for emission of one metric ton of carbon dioxide fell from a high of 24 euros, to about two euros.

Where, in Germany and Scandinavia, the elimination of nuclear power was added to this carbon trading and wind-solar subsidizing policy, the result was large increases in coal electricity as well as wind and solar; electricity prices three times those in the United States;

Lord Nicholas Stern (inset) directed Europe in 2004, as Al Gore directed a joint session of the U.S. Congress in 2012: "Put a price on carbon." The result was a continuing series of tax-evasion and securities swindles, corporate land-grabs in developing countries, and increasing emissions of air pollution in Europe.

Michelle Rasmusssen/EIR News Service

Creative Commons/Tom Raftery

increasingly unstable electricity grids: high profits for lowering economic productivity.

Carbon Crime

The constant throughout the rise and collapse of the carbon trading markets was crime: fraud, tax evasion, money-laundering, even support to terrorism.

In a typical case, London police in June 2010 arrested officials of Carbon Harvesting Corp. Ltd. a "carbon developer" launched by Barclays Bank, and charged them with a scheme to bribe Liberian officials to rent a fifth of Liberia's forests and profit by selling the credits that could be obtained from the carbon-absorbing trees.

Already in 2011, a German court jailed six traders over a 300 million euro fraud selling carbon emission permits through Deutsche Bank; a prelude to this month's bigger charges. The European law enforcement agency Europol estimated in 2010 that tax fraud associated with carbon trading cost governments $6.5 billion over 18 months, and that in some countries, up to 90% of total carbon trading volume was a result of fraudulent activities. Europol said that organized criminal syndicates were using the cash they earned from this type of carbon trading to fund other illicit activities in Europe, including cigarette smuggling, drug smuggling, and human trafficking.

In that year, Friends of the Earth even published a "manual" of the problem: "10 Ways To Game the Carbon-Trading Market." Michelle Chan of Friends of the Earth said, "Fraud and malfeasance are going to occur, and that's why we're skeptical of having a very Wall Street-driven, very liberalized market that basically is open to any and all comers."

In September 2014, Milan prosecutors concluded an investigation on a group of firms that stole over one billion euros through a carbon certificates scam to finance terrorism. The central figure is Imran Yakub Ahmed, a Pakistani with British passport, head of the Milan-based "SF Energy Trading", which bought CO2 certificates tax-free and sold them with a 20% VAT tax, which it kept. The gain was used to finance terrorism. The money went through European banks (including Deutsche Bank and the British Queen's own Coutts Bank) to Cyprus and Hong Kong, with Dubai as final destination.

The Milan investigators concluded that the European carbon trading markets are "strongly manipulated and flawed by an extraordinary number of commercial transactions activated to the precise aim of committing major fiscal frauds".

Der Spiegel reported an identical CO2 fraud scheme being investigated in Germany on June 7, 2014. Deutsche Bank played a key role, as it exported the carbon credits from Frankfurt to its London office (free of value-added tax or VAT), whence they were then traded elsewhere with VAT. The VAT, however, was never paid.

U.S. 'Green Disease' Spread After Kennedys and King Were Eliminated

by Marcia Merry Baker

In 1948 the Conservation Foundation was set up in Washington, D.C., as a continuation of the Hitler-era European-based eugenics and nature societies also active in America. The first director of the Foundation was Henry Fairfield Osborn, Jr. (1887-1969), whose father was a co-founder of the American Eugenics Society in 1926. The Conservation Foundation began a very active agenda, using code-language to avoid master-race taint, to promote pessimism and the unscientific bunk, that resources are limited and population must be curbed.

The Conservation Foundation is a marker of how a battery of initiatives—conferences, books, articles, university courses, etc.—was set loose in the United States in the post-WWII period, by leading British and trans-Atlantic race science advocates, to impose their evil program. The "enemy" to these networks, was the traditional American presumption, reinforced by the FDR years, that scientific, cultural and economic advancement can and must be achieved, forever. Population growth is a blessing.

Kingston(N.Y.) Leader 1-25-15

Mrs. E. H. Harriman Heads Movement to Stop the Early Weddings

American Genetic Association, whose committee on eugenics is headed by Mrs. E. H. [illegible] an extended study of the laws of heredity and some important facts have been developed. In its organ, the Journal of Heredity, the question "Does Early Marriage Lead to the Production of Undesirable Children?" was discussed some months ago by Mr. Redfield of Chicago who in connection with his article offered a reward of $200 to any person "finding a case of a superior human being produced by a rapid breeding;" that is by breeding faster than three generations to a century.

The reward has not been claimed and Mr. Redfield now presents a table to prove his contention that marriages are not desirable. He says "In 23 states the legal age of marriage ranges from 16 to 19 years for boys, and from 13 to 17 for girls. In the same states there are many mariages at less than legal age which are considered valid unless objection is made. Such early marriages result in rapid generations, and continuous rapid generations lead to the production of mental and moral defectives."

So important a matter, affecting as it does the well-being and progress of the race, deserves more attention than it has been receiving. Persons in their teens, carried away by romance and disposed to elope, need to heed the advice of their parents, who almost invariably oppose early marriage, not for scientific reasons, which may vitally concern society, but because they want their children to realize the responsibilities involved in the step they contemplate and realization can come only with years, experience and knowledge. They do not want their children "tied down" too early in life for economic and social reasons. They feel the nearer their children

N.Y.World 9-5-15

MRS. E.H. HARRIMAN BACKS A GIGANTIC STEP IN EUGENICS

Would Curb Defectives Hundreds of Thousands Over Series of Years.

TO MAKE RACE PERFECT.

Aid of Rockefeller and Carnegie Hoped For in World Wide Campaign.

A world wide campaign for the sterilization of defectives is called for in a report to the Eugenic Society, which has headquarters at Cold Spring Harbor, L. I., and is generously aided financially by Mrs. E. H. Harriman. John D. Rockefeller and Andrew Carnegie are expected to contribute to the campaign.

The report to the society was prepared by the Committee on Sterilization and advocates such treatment for 82,400 persons in the United States in the next year. The number to be sterilized the report says, should be increased annually until, by 1980, when it will have reached 415,000.

At that time, it is predicted, these and other measures looking to the improvement of the race will have brought about very nearly perfect men and women.

Statistics prepared by the society show that 10 per cent. of the total population is made up of defectives.

The members of the Sterilization Committee of the society are Bleeker Van Wagenen, H. H. Laughlin, W. M. Carmalt, New Haven; Everett Flood, Palmer, Mass., and H. W. Mitchell, Warren, Pa.

The Eugenic Society's resident director is Dr. Charles B. Davenport, biologist, of this city. Concerning the sterilization phase of eugenic work he

BK:HAR-2 _ 44

Portland(Ore) Journal 9-11-15

Mrs. E. H. Harriman is backing a campaign by the Eugenic society, the object of which is to produce the perfect man in 1980. Presumably the perfect woman will arrive at the same time, provided she isn't already here.

The Harrimans and Rockefellers were blatant about their intentions—as is made clear in this clipping from the New York World, Sept. 3, 1915. Following World War II, their eugenics turned "green."

Progress—Enemy to the Greens

In practice, this human American outlook was in effect during the 1940s through the early 1960s in many areas. Nuclear power as the coming new energy mode was seen in the 1956 opening of the first commercial nuclear reactor, in western Pennsylvania. Soon there were dozens of orders for reactors. In 1953 President Eisenhower announced the Atoms for Peace program, committed to the nuclear era to uplift all mankind.

The Green Revolution plant-breeding program was making great strides. A team of Mexican, Indian and other researchers, led by American scientist Norman Borlaug, developed new strains of corn and wheat, to the point that Mexico in the 1960s was a grain exporter, and India became food self-sufficient by 1974. The prospect was on the horizon, of even better and faster plant-life upgrading and protection from pests through use of genetic engineering and radiation methods.

There were dramatic achievements against long-standing human diseases. Malaria, the centuries-old scourge, was dramatically reduced by the use of DDT to repel and kill the mosquito vector, beginning in the

1940s. Vaccines were developed against poliomyelitis, measles and other debilitating and widespread illnesses.

Large-scale water management projects were underway and under discussion. The California State Water Project, constructed from 1960 to 1973, was a statewide system of 21 major dams and 1,100 km of conduits, to re-distribute scarce water in the state across three river basins. The North American Water and Power Alliance, the continental scale project, was presented to Congress favorably in 1964. Mexico and the United States were conducting joint research for nuclear desalination.

These successes, and the love for humanity behind them, were anathema to the royalist green crowd. Their propaganda against human advancement took, first, the general theme that the Earth's "limited" resources must be "conserved"—even "undisturbed"—by cutting back on people and their activities. And secondly, there were specific propaganda salvos contrived to counter individual advances.

In September, 1983, the Club of Life book was released, There Are No Limits to Growth *by Lyndon H. LaRouche, Jr., developing proofs circulated over the previous decade that the Club of Rome's* Limits to Growth *was scientifically fraudulent.*

Green Onslaught

The latter operations included such campaigns as the anti-DDT campaign, claiming that it and other modern chemicals pollute. The anti-nuclear campaign claimed that radiation is inherently dangerous. The anti-crop improvement campaign claimed that genetic alterations—especially by bio-technology—were inherently dangerous. The anti-water management campaign claimed that ecology—wildlife habitat—was threatened by water impoundment and transfer, especially intermingling water across river basins. The anti-vaccine campaign claimed that inocculation is either inherently dangerous, or deliberately tainted, or both. And so on.

All the while, the generalized, green anti-population onslaught included such initiatives as the 1952 establishment of the Population Council in the U.S., whose founding meeting included Fairfield Osborn, and his relative, Frederick Henry Osborn, the eugenicist. Principal funding was from the John D. Rockefeller Foundation. The wave of propaganda over the 1950s-'60s featured such writings as the 1953 book, *The Limits of the Earth*, by Fairfield Osborn.

In 1961, the newly-founded, royalist World Wildlife Fund set up its American headquarters in Washington, D.C., in offices adjoining the Conservation Foundation. Operating as one, the two entities formally merged in 1985, under the WWF name. In 1961, the new president of the Conservation Foundation was William K. Reilly, who, in 1985, became head of the WWF in the United States. Reilly's mentor was Russell Train, President of the WWF (1978-1985) and then its Board Chairman (1985-1994). Both went on to hold top formal green positions in government, on Nixon's Council on Environmental Quality (CEQ), at the Environmental Protection Agency, and other posts.

In 1963 came a critical deciding factor in the success of these networks to subvert the United States: President John F. Kennedy was assassinated. His presidency had furthered economy-building, scientific optimism for mankind's future, especially the Apollo Lunar program and commitment to nuclear power and space. Eliminating him, along with the assassination of Martin Luther King, Jr., Senator Robert Kennedy, and others, was part of a terrible national downshift in that decade. The interconnecting networks responsible for these crimes include the green subversives.

1970 Earth Day—the Marker

The establishment of "Earth Day" in 1970, was a marker for the success of green ideology making its way into Federal law, agency regulations and thinking. For example, in 1969, new Federal law forbade state efforts to study or undertake transfer of water between river basins. In December 1970, the Environmental Protection Agency (EPA) came into being, with a mandate to decide for each of its 10 geographic regions, what human activity is acceptable for the "environment." In 1972, the first head of the EPA, William Ruckelshaus, banned the use of DDT in the United States, on bogus claims—which he later admitted—that it was potentially harmful.

The 1972 book *Limits to Growth*, released by the Club of Rome, was the touchstone for this deadly greening process. It was a trashy fraud, based on a computer model by two Americans, Dennis Meadows and Jay Forrester, asserting that the boundary condition of Earth's resource base for humans would be reached in 100 years. However, thanks to a heavy public relations push, the book sold 30 million copies, in multiple languages.

EPA

William K. Reilly, EPA Administrator (1989-1992) for George H.W. Bush, was a careerist for the green agenda, serving in various government positions through to the Obama Administration, and as head of the World Wildlife Fund, and the Conservation Foundation.

Americans were told to "cut back," and "conserve." President Jimmy Carter, on April 18, 1977, appeared in a sweater, on a televised speech, telling Americans that the White House had turned down the thermostat, and they too, must conserve fuel. Nuclear power was singled out for demonization and cancellation. In 1979, an accident at the Three Mile Island, Pennsylvania nuclear plant—with no ill effects—was nevertheless used as a scare, after which, "environmental" requirements made building nuclear reactors nearly impossible.

The U.S. economic decline has been unceasing. Nuclear reactor plans and orders, which at their peak numbered 243, were cancelled in mass numbers, so the United States ended up in 2000, with only 104 plants, now aging, in operation. There is no nuclear desalination whatsoever, except on Navy vessels. The U.S. productive workforce (goods manufacture, construction, mining, transportation, power utilities and engineering) has fallen in absolute numbers from 26.8 million in 1970, down to 25.1 million today. The United States is 30% import-dependent for food, overall. The decrepit condition of bridges, highways and urban infrastructure is notorious. As of 2000, for the first time in a century, American infectious disease rates began to rise. The 2010 census showed that life expectancy is going down, including for women, in dozens of the 3,000 U.S. counties, in poor parts of the country. California, and nearby parts of the Southwest—nearly 50 million people—face running out of water in a year. The NASA space program has been downsized to dysfunction levels.

Global Warming Hoax Imposed

A special impetus for this breakdown process came 40 years ago, with the 1975 confab at Research Triangle Park, North Carolina, of depopulation activists, who came up with the mother of all scare stories: manmade global warming. The scenario is that mankind's emissions of carbon dioxide, methane and other substances, constitute "greenhouse gases" which are over-heating the planet. Thus man's activities and numbers must be cut. Imposing this hoax has been carried through to the present, especially by the Bush and Obama presidencies, not to mention Al Gore doing his part.

George Herbert Walker Bush was active and outspoken on this de-population goal, all during his pre-White House years. This was in line with his father before him, banker Prescott Bush, who backed Hitler and justified his support as purely "commercial."

During G.H.W. Bush's two terms in Congress (1966-1970), he led it to approve the creation of a Commission on Population Growth and the American Future, for which John D. Rockeller III became the first chairman in 1969. Bush helped found, then chair, the Republican Task Force on Earth Resources and Population, churning out a steady stream of propaganda claiming that the world was over-populated, and that the fixed limit to resources was close at hand. This provided a public forum for even outright race-science.

Witnesses included Paul Ehrlich, founder of Zero Population Growth, as well as Gen. William Draper, then Chairman of the Population Crisis Committee, which originated in 1965, to promote, as he said, "culling the human herd." Draper was a close friend of Bush's father, Prescott.

In 1969, Bush brought in race scientists William Shockley and Arthur Jensen to testify, asserting that

Soybean Board of Nebraska

In the diversion of U.S. food and feed crops for fuel, there is a push for soybean bio-diesel, as well as corn ethanol, as shown in this Nebraska promotion bus.

blacks were genetically inferior to whites in intelligence. Bush himself said, in his follow-up summation, that Dr. Shockley's expertise was important to present "the facts about hereditary aspects of human quality. Furthermore, he [Dr. Shockley] claimed our well-intentioned social welfare programs may be unwittingly producing a downbreeding of the quality of the U.S. population." Bush warned poor, black people, "that they cannot hope to acquire a larger share of American prosperity without cutting down on births."

During the George H.W. Bush Presidency (1989-1993), there were repeated assertions about the danger of global warming. Obama has met repeatedly with leading British green nabobs. Within days of Obama's 2009 inauguration, Sir Nicholas Stern was in Washington, D.C. He had issued the 2006 "Stern Review Report on the Economics of Climate Change," presenting how human activity should be cut back by "markets" (carbon credits, trading, etc.) and government (carbon taxes and limits).

In May, 2015, Obama fawningly spoke on BBC TV with David Attenborough, the infamous British naturalist who denounces humanity. Attenborough said in 2011, when receiving an award from his friend Prince Philip: "We now realize that the disasters that continue increasingly to afflict the natural world have one element that connects them all—the unprecedented increase in the number of human beings on this planet."

In December, 2009, Obama's EPA officially declared that carbon dioxide (which humans exhale, and plants breathe in) is a dangerous pollutant; and designated five other gases likewise. This opened the way for top-down agency orders against the economy, under statutes of the Clean Air Act of 1970. Coal became the enemy. On Aug. 3, 2015 Obama and the EPA announced their "Clean Power Plan," which calls for cutting carbon emission from power plants by 30% by the year 2030, compared to 2005—the first ever such decree based on statutory authority alone. Already, 15 states have filed suit against it. The power base of the United States is in shambles. By 2014 natural gas exceeded coal in share of U.S. electricity generation. Nuclear is contracting.

Obama praised his new Clean Power Plan as, "the biggest, most important step we've ever taken to combat climate change." He plans a high-profile trip to the Alaskan Arctic at the end of August and a September meeting with Pope Francis, as part of his climate change awareness campaign, for a global treaty in December.

The green subversion record is clear.

www.ingramcontent.com/pod-product-compliance
Ingram Content Group UK Ltd.
Pitfield, Milton Keynes, MK11 3LW, UK
UKHW050147280726
14058UKWH00007B/886